RAT'S WARS

Other *Pearls Before Swine* Collections

Unsportsmanlike Conduct
Because Sometimes You Just Gotta Draw a Cover with Your Left Hand
Larry in Wonderland
When Pigs Fly
50,000,000 Pearls Fans Can't Be Wrong
The Saturday Evening Pearls
Macho Macho Animals
The Sopratos
Da Brudderhood of Zeeba Zeeba Eata
The Ratvolution Will Not Be Televised
Nighthogs
This Little Piggy Stayed Home
BLTs Taste So Darn Good

Treasuries

Pearls Freaks the #%# Out*
Pearls Blows Up
Pearls Sells Out
The Crass Menagerie
Lions and Tigers and Crocs, Oh My!
Sgt. Piggy's Lonely Hearts Club Comic

Gift Books

Friends Should Know When They're Not Wanted
Da Crockydile Book o' Frendsheep

amp! Comics for Kids

Beginning Pearls

A *Pearls Before Swine* Collection

by Stephan Pastis

Andrews McMeel
Publishing, LLC
Kansas City • Sydney • London

Pearls Before Swine is distributed internationally by Universal Uclick.

Andrews McMeel Publishing, LLC
an Andrews McMeel Universal company
1130 Walnut Street, Kansas City, Missouri 64106

www.andrewsmcmeel.com

13 14 15 16 17 SHO 10 9 8 7 6 5 4 3 2 1

ISBN: 978-1-4494-2936-2

Library of Congress Control Number: 2013930114

Pearls Before Swine can be viewed on the Internet at
www.pearlscomic.com

These strips appeared in newspapers from December 5, 2011, to September 2, 2012.

Dedication

To Tom Richmond and Jeff Keane, for letting me mock them in this book's introduction.

(Alright, fine. They didn't have a choice.)

Introduction

When you've just flown thirteen hours on a C-17 into Kandahar, Afghanistan, these are not the first words you want to hear as you get off the plane:

"Good news, boys. The base has not been attacked in three weeks."

But that's how our military escort greeted us.

And that, to me, did not sound like good news.

But there I was, on a USO-sponsored trip to visit the troops in Afghanistan, surrounded by fellow cartoonists Mike Luckovich (editorial cartoonist for the *Atlanta Journal Constitution*), Jeff Keane (*Family Circus*), Rick Kirkman (*Baby Blues*), Garry Trudeau (*Doonesbury*), and Tom Richmond (*Mad Magazine*).

Our military escorts immediately split us up into two groups. Garry, Rick, and Mike went to eat at the dining facility. And Jeff, Tom, and I went to check out the bunks in our living quarters.

Now despite the rather profound tonal differences between *Pearls* and *Family Circus*, the fact is that Jeff Keane and I are brothers in a very small fraternity of 200. That's the number of syndicated cartoonists in the United States.

But not Tom. His expertise is caricatures. And as we all know, caricaturists are a dime a dozen.

Why, just look at his barely passable artwork:

So it was only appropriate that when they assigned us to our rooms, the military put Jeff and me in one room and Tom in another.

Jeff immediately took the big bed.

Leaving me with the not-so-big bunk bed.

But that was okay. We were brothers in syndication.

And besides, I'd make up for it by ripping on *Family Circus* in some future *Pearls* strip.

And then our good luck ended.

With a loud air raid siren.

"GET DOWN! GET DOWN! GET DOWN!" shouted a man over the base's P.A. system.

The door of our room burst open.

"You boys need to get your gear on fast," said our military escort, now standing in his bare feet. "The base is under attack."

And faster than you can say, "Not me, Mommy!," the creator of *Family Circus* and I put on our armored vests and helmets.

And as we did, our military escort tried to comfort us.

I, of course, didn't need it. Jeff, on the other, was running around in circles, leaving his trademark dotted-line.

"The first thing you need to know is that we have a blast wall on this side of the building," our escort said, pointing to the west side of the structure. "And a blast wall on the far side of the building," he said, pointing to the east side.

Photo of blast wall.

"So," he added, "if the rocket that was just fired lands on either the east side of us or the west side of us, you're fine. The blast wall will absorb the impact."

I immediately felt reassured.

"I should note, however," he continued, "that we do have what is known as a soft roof. That means that if the rocket were to hit right on top of us, well. . . ." His voice trailed off and he shrugged his shoulders.

I immediately felt un-reassured.

So as the sirens wailed and the P.A. system shouted, "GET DOWN," I waited there with the creator of *Family Circus* for whatever would happen next, not sure what I feared more—death, or the fact that the last thing I would see on earth was the creator of *Family Circus*.

And after the longest minute of my life, the sirens disappeared.

Where the rocket hit, we never knew. The base was, after all, the size of a small city.

All we knew was that the escort told us we could take off our gear.

And so Jeff and I took off our gear, high-fiving each other like two kids on the last day of school.

And that's when we remembered Tom.

Throughout the entire episode, neither the military escort, nor Jeff, nor I, thought to alert the cartoonist down the hall.

Who, with iPod earbuds in his ears, had absolutely no idea what was happening around him.

That's right.

Tom Richmond heard neither the sirens, nor the "GET DOWN," nor the sound of Jeff Keane scampering around in little circles.

Now the good news is that had the rocket actually hit our building, Tom never would have known what happened. His last moment on earth would have been filled with whatever Britney Spears song he was undoubtedly bobbing his head to.

And besides, he learned a valuable lesson:

When the bombs start dropping, we cartoonists stick together.

We *syndicated* cartoonists.

Because—as even our military escort knew,

. . . the caricaturists are a dime a dozen.

Stephan Pastis
October, 2013

HEY, DAD, WHY'S YOUR PAL BOB IN THE BATHROOM?
He changing clothes. Gonna dress like person from City Planning Deepartment. Tell zeeba he have to tear down beeg wall around property.

DOES HE REALLY RESEMBLE A PERSON?
Peese, son. No eensult us.
12/5

Yeah. No eensult us.
Whoa. Reesemblance uncanny.

WHY DO ALL OF THESE OBITUARIES ALWAYS SAY THAT SO-AND-SO 'PASSED AWAY PEACEFULLY'?
WHAT DO YOU MEAN, 'WHY?' BECAUSE THE PERSON DIED PEACEFULLY.
THE TIMES

YEAH, WELL, WHEN I DIE, I'M GONNA GO OUT PUNCHING NURSES AND DOCTORS, JUST SO SOMEONE CAN FINALLY SAY, 'HE PASSED AWAY VIOLENTLY.'

THE TIMES
12/6

WHAT A GOAL.
BRING IT ON, DEATH!

HEY, RAT, I'D LIKE YOU TO MEET MY FRIEND, BOB. HE'S A MECHANICAL ENGINEER. YOU'LL HAVE TO EXCUSE HIM, THOUGH... HE THINKS HE'S MISSING SOMETHING.
12/7

CHARISMA?

MY KEYS.
MY MISTAKE.
WOMEN MUST SURE LOVE ALL THOSE PENCILS, BOB.

YOU EVER HAVE ONE OF THOSE DAYS WHERE YOUR BRAIN JUST DOESN'T SEEM TO BE FUNCTIONING CORRECTLY?

BONK
BONK
BONK
12/8

WORKS WITH THE T.V.

I GET SO TIRED OF UNMOTIVATED PEOPLE SOMETIMES. HOW CAN SOMEONE HAVE NO PASSION IN LIFE? NO RAISON D'ETRE?
OH, I'VE GOT SOME OF THAT.

THAT'S RAISIN *BRAN*.
Raisin Bran
12/9

IT'S 'A REASON FOR EXISTENCE.'
NOT REALLY, BUT IT'S A PRETTY GOOD CEREAL.

WHERE IS PIG?
READING THE NEWSPAPER ON MY iPad. HE WAS FASCINATED THAT THE WHOLE NEWSPAPER WAS ON SUCH AN EASY-TO-READ DEVICE.
12/10

WELL, HOW WAS IT?
GREAT! I READ THE WHOLE NEWSPAPER!

WHERE'S THE iPad?
I USED IT TO LINE MY BIRD CAGE.

GUESS HE DOESN'T LIKE BIRDS.

HEY, PIG, WHAT DO YOU NEED?
I'M THE TAPPING PIG! I GO DOOR-TO-DOOR TAP DANCING FOR PEOPLE AND THEN KEEP TRACK OF WHETHER OR NOT THEY LIKED IT. SO FAR, EVERYONE'S LOVED IT!

LISTEN, PIG, I HAVEN'T HAD A CHANCE TO TALK TO YOU, BUT I GOT SOME BAD NEWS LAST NIGHT. MY COUSIN DEAN WAS EATEN BY LIONS.

AND WHEN THEY WERE DONE, THEY ATE MY UNCLE STEVE. THEN HIS BROTHER PETE.

A WHOLE FAMILY WIPED OUT BY A GROUP OF HEARTLESS, INSATIABLE PREDATORS...WHEN DOES IT END?...WHEN DOES THE MINDLESS VIOLENCE AND SUFFERING OF THIS WORLD END?!?

TAPPITY
TAPPITY
TAP TAP
TAP
12/11

☑ **Not a fan.**

DO YOU EVER MEET A PERSON AND KNOW IMMEDIATELY YOU'RE NOT GONNA LIKE THEM?
OH, SURE.

YEAH...WHAT IS IT ABOUT CERTAIN PEOPLE THAT TELLS YOU THAT?
THEY'RE BREATHING.
12/12

MAYBE YOU'RE THE WRONG GUY TO ASK.
AND MOUTHS. THEY ALL SEEM TO HAVE MOUTHS.

WHAT ARE YOU DOING, PIG?
PLANNING A PARTY AT MY HOUSE, BUT I NEED SOME GAMES WHERE PEOPLE CAN WIN PARTY BAGS. DO YOU KNOW ANY GOOD GAMES?

DO THE ONE WHERE YOU PUT PENNIES IN A JAR, AND SEE WHO CAN COME THE CLOSEST TO GUESSING HOW MANY ARE IN THERE.
OOH, GREAT IDEA.
12/13

THREE.
YOU ARE *REALLY* GOOD AT THIS.

BEFORE TODAY'S PERFORMANCE OF 'PEARLS,' WE'D APPRECIATE IT IF ALL OF YOU READERS WOULD PLEASE TURN OFF YOUR CELL PHONES SO AS TO NOT INTERFERE WITH OTHER READERS' VIEWING ENJOYMENT. THANK YOU....

HEY, RAT, WHERE WERE YOU LAST NIGHT?
A MONKEY IN PANTS STOLE MY—
Riiiiiinng
Riiiiiing
Riiiiiinng
Riiiiiing
12/14

IT'S THE GUY IN CLEVELAND AGAIN!
USHER, PLEASE REMOVE THE CLEVELAND MAN.
HIM AGAIN?!

IF THAT READER IN CLEVELAND IS GONNA INTERRUPT OUR STRIP BY NOT TURNING OFF HIS CELL PHONE WHILE HE READS THE NEWSPAPER, I'M GONNA RUIN HIS DAY RIGHT BACK!
HOW YOU GONNA DO THAT?

FOUR DOWN IS 'EVE'!!
12/15

YOU REALLY SHOULDN'T GIVE AWAY THE CROSSWORD.
KEEP IT UP, PAL....THE SUDOKU'S NEXT!!

WHAT ARE YOU LOOKING AT, DAD?
Crocs climb zeeba wall. Now dey juss need way geet down into zeeba yard.
12/16

HOW ARE THEY GONNA DO IT?
Dey essperimenting.

So much for 'pusheeng Bob.'

HEY, YOU'RE 'PIG' FROM THE COMIC STRIP 'PEARLS BEFORE SWINE'!...MIND SIGNING MY 'PEARLS' BOOK?
SURE! WHAT'S YOUR NAME?

STACEY... WITH AN 'EY.'
GOTCHA!
12/17

TO STEYCI

T-SHIR
SHOP

I'M WITH STUPID

I'M WITH STUPID

I'M WITH STUPID

I'M WITH STUPID

I'M WITH STUPID

I'M STUPID
12/18

WHAT ARE YOU WATCHING, GOAT?
'IT'S A WONDERFUL LIFE.' IT'S A CLASSIC CHRISTMAS MOVIE.

IS THAT THE ONE WHERE THEY SAY, 'EVERY TIME A BELL RINGS, A PIG GETS BEATEN.'?
THAT'S NOT THE SAYING.

PLEASE DON'T RUIN THE FUN.
WHY IS THAT A CLASSIC?

WHERE WERE YOU GUYS?
SEEING THAT NEW 4D MOVIE.

4D? THE FOURTH DIMENSION IS TIME.
YEAH. THE MOVIE ENDS BEFORE IT STARTS.

NEVER MIND.
STRANGE THINGS HAPPEN IN THE FOURTH DIMENSION.
LOOK! MY POPCORN'S STILL WARM.

WHAT ARE YOU DRINKING, STEPH?
A NEW GERMAN BEER. IT'S GREAT.

GERMAN?! HA! I DRINK AN ALL-AMERICAN BEER WITH ITS RED, WHITE AND BLUE LABEL AND ITS ALL-AMERICAN ADS FILLED WITH AMERICAN FLAGS AND AMERICAN BARBECUES AND AMERICAN BASEBALL!!

THAT BEER YOU'RE HOLDING IS NOW OWNED BY A EUROPEAN COMPANY.

I KNEW THAT.

YOU HOPE TO ACCOMPLISH A LOT IN LIFE, RIGHT?
SURE. WHY?
12/22

BECAUSE I JUST FIGURED OUT THAT WITH YOU BEING 43 YEARS OLD, AND THE AVERAGE LIFE EXPECTANCY FOR A MAN BEING 76 YEARS OLD, YOUR LIFE IS AT LEAST 56 PERCENT OVER.
SO?

SO IF YOUR LIFE IS A FOOTBALL GAME, YOU'RE WELL INTO THE THIRD QUARTER AND DOWN 20 POINTS.

ARE YOU DONE?
LEMME GUESS.. YOU'RE BANKING ON A MIRACULOUS FOURTH QUARTER COMEBACK.
THROW A HAIL MARY, STEPH!

WHAT ARE YOU WRITING, PIG?
A BUCKET LIST OF ALL THE THINGS I'D LIKE TO DO BEFORE I DIE.

① Stand on it.
② Put it on head.
③ Roll it down street.
12/23

YOU KNOW, THINGS ON YOUR BUCKET LIST DON'T HAVE TO INVOLVE BUCKETS.
WHOA. NOW THAT BROADENS THINGS.

HEY, PIG, WHAT'S WRONG?
OHH, ZEBRA... I'VE BEEN HEARING VOICES.
12/24

REALLY?
REALLY.

WELL, LOOK... IT'S NOT THE END OF THE WORLD. WE'LL GET YOU HELP... A GOOD PSYCHOLOGIST.
HOW WILL THAT MAKE THE COUPLE NEXT DOOR STOP FIGHTING?

THOSE ARE YOUR VOICES?
HEY... WHAT CAN HE DO ABOUT THEIR BARKING DOG?

"Well now, there's a constellation you don't see every day."

For Bil Keane, 1922-2011

I'M HAVING A BAD DAY... A REAL BAD DAY.
DON'T BE DOWN, RAT. YOUR LIFE'S NOT *THAT* BAD. JUST ASK THE SPECTRAL TORTOISE O' PERSPECTIVE.
12/26

YOU COULD BE DEAD.

HE'S QUITE THE PICKER-UPPER.

Okay, guys, we is wait here for zeeba neighba. When he show up, Bob smash heem wid rock.
How long we got wait?
Long as it take.

12/27

TOSS
THUD
Me got bored.

HEY, GOAT... WANT TO PLAY BADMINTON WITH ME AND PIG? YOU JUST TAKE A RACKET AND HIT THIS LITTLE THINGIE.
YOUR LITTLE THINGIE THERE IS CALLED A 'SHUTTLECOCK.'
12/28

WHAP

SOMEHOW I DIDN'T LIKE THE SOUND OF THAT.

Look... It shifty leetle rat. Mebbe he got idea how crocs can geet down eento zeeba yard.

DUDE. JUST GO DOWN A LADDER.

Any more idea?
12/29

HEY, NEIGHBOR BOB...WHAT'S THE MATTER WITH YOU?
I DUNNO. JUST BEEN REAL DOWN LATELY. I NEED A REAL SHOT IN THE ARM.
12/30

BLAM

DID THAT HELP?

12/31

TOOOOT

PEARLS
10th
Anniversary
12/31/01 -
12/31/11

SOMEHOW I EXPECTED MORE.
CAN I GO HOME NOW?

Elly Elephant was sick of Henry Hippo.

So she sat in her kitchen and tried to envision her dream man.

"I will take this empty basket and put in one avocado for each trait I want in a man."

So she put in one avocado for sensitivity, and one for handsome, and one for adventurous.

"And I want him to be dependable," she said, putting in another avocado. But when she did, out fell adventurous.

"Well, he at least needs to be non-superficial," she said, adding another avocado. But out dropped handsome.

"Okay, he can't be needy," she said, squeezing in another. But out fell sensitive.

"The basket can't hold all the avocados," Elly cried in despair. "I'll simply have to learn to be happy with the few avocados I have."

Which was none because Henry Hippo turned them into guacamole.

GUARD DUCK STARTED PLAYING BINGO WITH THE SENIORS AT THE RETIREMENT CENTER.
WHY BINGO?

DOCTOR SAID HE HAS HIGH BLOOD PRESSURE. IT'S SUPPOSED TO HELP HIM RELAX.
THAT'S GREAT. HOW'S HE DOING WITH IT?

NO, I DO NOT WANT TO FORM A BINGO ALLIANCE.

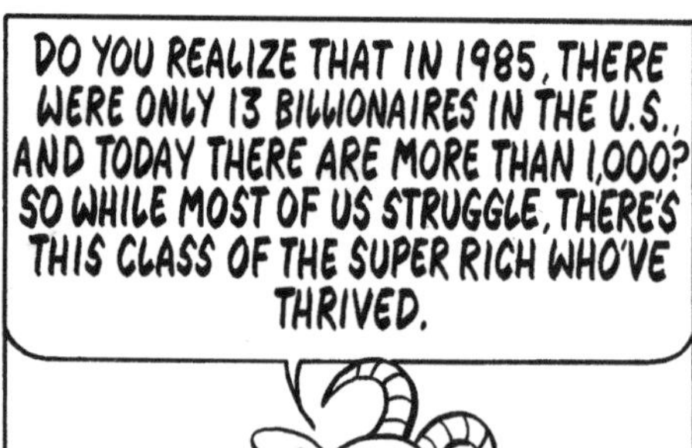
DO YOU REALIZE THAT IN 1985, THERE WERE ONLY 13 BILLIONAIRES IN THE U.S., AND TODAY THERE ARE MORE THAN 1,000? SO WHILE MOST OF US STRUGGLE, THERE'S THIS CLASS OF THE SUPER RICH WHO'VE THRIVED.

THAT'S NOT FAIR. WE NEED TO CHANGE THAT.
I AGREE. BUT HOW?

BY JOINING THAT CLASS.
I THINK YOU'RE MISSING THE POINT.
LET ME BE ONE OF YOU, RICH PEOPLE!

THE CROCS ARE ASKING THE CITY TO TEAR DOWN YOUR WALL ON THE GROUND THAT IT POSES A DANGER TO CHILDREN.
HOW DO THEY FIGURE THAT?

THEY SAY A HELPLESS CHILD COULD CLIMB ON TOP AND SUFFER A TRAGIC FALL.
BUT THAT'S NEVER HAPPENED. AND THEY HAVE NO PROOF IT EVER WOULD.

Why me got wear funny costume, Bob?
Shut mouf and walk closer to edge, Burt.

LOOK WHAT I BOUGHT, RAT...IT'S THE 'MOUNTED BUFFALO HEAD OF REGRET.'
WHAT'S THE REGRET?

NOT DUCKING.

IT'S REALLY LIMITED HIS OPTIONS.

1/5

HEY, RAT, I'M TRYING TO SET UP THAT POKER GAME YOU ASKED FOR, BUT I DON'T KNOW WHO TO INVITE.
WHO CARES? WE JUST NEED PLAYERS. ASK ANYONE WITH ARMS THAT CAN HOLD CARDS.

THAT HURTS.

TRY TO BE MORE SENSITIVE AROUND MR. BUFFALO HEAD.

1/6

WHAT'S THE MATTER, PIG?
MY STUPID COMPUTER. IF I DON'T USE AN ANTI-VIRUS PROGRAM, I GET SOME RUSSIAN-MADE VIRUS ON MY COMPUTER THAT STEALS MY CREDIT CARD NUMBER.

BUT IF I DO USE AN ANTI-VIRUS PROGRAM, IT SLOWS MY COMPUTER DOWN TO A CRAWL AND INTERRUPTS EVERYTHING I DO WITH STUPID MESSAGES.

YEAH, BUT WHAT CAN YOU DO?
I E-MAILED MY CREDIT CARD NUMBER TO THE RUSSIANS.

IT'S A BIG TIME-SAVER.

1/7

WHAT ARE YOU SUPPOSED TO BE?
VITO CORLEONE. I'M GOING TO A MOB COSTUME PARTY.

A MOB COSTUME PARTY?
YEAH. AND THIS IS A STATUE OF JIMMY HOFFA. GUARD DUCK MADE IT FOR ME. I BRING ONE EVERY YEAR.

WHAT FOR?
AT THE END OF THE PARTY, THE MOBSTERS BLOW IT UP. THERE'S A LITTLE FUSE IN HIS HEAD. BUT I THINK WE NEED TO CHANGE THE DESIGN.
WHY IS THAT?

BECAUSE PEOPLE ARE ALWAYS RE-DOING THE FUSE TO MAKE IT SHORTER. THAT WAY IT BLOWS UP RIGHT WHEN THEY LIGHT IT.
BUT THAT'S NOT SAFE.

I KNOW. THAT'S WHY I'M CHANGING IT.
WHAT ARE YOU GONNA DO?

1/8

I'M GONNA MAKE THEM A HOFFA THEY CAN'T RE-FUSE.

WHY IS EVERYONE GOING TO THESE 'OCCUPY WALL STREET' PROTESTS?
BECAUSE THEY VIEW IT AS THE CENTER OF CORPORATE GREED.
1/9

BUT WHAT ABOUT ALL THE OTHER STREETS IN NEW YORK? WE SHOULD BE PROTESTING ON THOSE, TOO.
WHICH ONES DO YOU SUGGEST?

OCCUPY SESAME STREET
PLEASE LEAVE.
SHUT YOUR FACE, GROVER.

I CAN'T BELIEVE YOU'RE PROTESTING 'SESAME STREET.'
YOU CAN'T, HUH?..WELL, THINK ABOUT IT...
OCCUPY SESAME STREET
1/10

THE SHOW TEACHES YOUNG PEOPLE THAT THE 99% OF AMERICANS WHO ARE NOT RICH HAVE NO CHOICE BUT TO GET USED TO THEIR SUBSTANDARD LIVING CONDITIONS.
WHAT ARE YOU TALKING ABOUT ?!

Hey kids, It's fun to live in garbage cans.
SEE?
HEY, C'MON, HE'S GROUCHY ABOUT IT.

THIS PROTEST IS STUPID.
STUPID? THERE'S AN ENTIRE GENERATION OF YOUNG MEN OUT THERE WHO CAN'T GET JOBS. SO INSTEAD OF BUYING HOMES AND STARTING FAMILIES, THEY'RE STUCK LIVING WITH FRIENDS IN CRAPPY, ONE-ROOM APARTMENTS.
OCCUPY SESAME STREET
1/11

FINE. BUT WHAT'S THAT HAVE TO DO WITH 'SESAME STREET'??
THEY PROMOTE IT.
PROMOTE IT *HOW*?!

Bert and I would like to go to sleep now.
PIPE DOWN, YOU BRAINWASHING MUPPET.
OCCUPY SESAME

RAT GAVE UP HIS 'SESAME STREET' PROTEST.
HOW COME?

PBS AGREED TO LET HIM REVIVE ONE OF THEIR OLD CHILDREN'S SHOWS.
RAT HOSTING A CHILDREN'S SHOW? WHICH ONE?

PLEASE DON'T YOU BE MY NEIGHBOR...

Okay, zeeba neighba, crocs has new stratagee. We ees smash you wid rock. Me say where to throw. Burt throw. Dat prove we great team. Dat prove we work togedder. Dat—

CRACK

Speech go on leetle long.

WHAT'S THE MATTER WITH YOU?
I CAN'T FIND MY CELL PHONE ANYWHERE. I THINK I LEFT IT IN THE DINER. ZEBRA'S THERE NOW, SO I'M TELLING HIM WHERE TO LOOK FOR IT.

WHAT'S THAT IN YOUR HAND?

GET HELP.

LOOKS LIKE ONE OF YOUR NEIGHBORS GOT HIMSELF APPOINTED TO THE CITY PLANNING COMMISSION.
TRIBUNE
1/15

WHAT'S THAT?
THEY'RE THE GUYS WHO ISSUE PERMITS FOR ANY CONSTRUCTION YOU WANT TO DO.

THEY DON'T BY CHANCE HAVE THE RIGHT TO TEAR DOWN STUFF YOU BUILD WITHOUT A PERMIT, DO THEY?

SURE THEY DO. THEY JUST BRING OVER THE WRECKING BALL AND DOWN IT GOES. WHY?
TRIBUNE

WEEEEEEEE
CITY PLANN

IF YOU'LL EXCUSE ME, I HAVE A WALL PERMIT TO FILE FOR.
WALL? WHAT WALL?

YOU EVER NOTICE HOW SOME OF THE OLDER COMIC STRIPS ALWAYS HAVE A WIDE-EYED OPEN-MOUTHED GUY IN THE LAST PANEL?
YEAH. IT'S A VISUAL CUE SO THE READER KNOWS HE'S JUST READ THE PUNCHLINE.

WHY DON'T YOUR STRIPS HAVE THAT?
I DON'T KNOW... I GUESS I HOPE THE JOKE IS WELL WRITTEN ENOUGH THAT THE READER DOESN'T NEED AN OBVIOUS CUE LIKE THAT.

!

WHOA... NOW I GET THIS STUPID STRIP.
GET RID OF HIM.
ZOINKS!

WHAT HAPPENED TO YOU, STEPH?
I FLEW FROM L.A. TO OAKLAND AND THE AIRLINE LOST MY LUGGAGE. IT HAD ALL MY CLOTHES, MY HAT, MY CONTACT LENSES. THEY HAVE NO IDEA WHERE IT IS.

OH, NO, STEPH... WAS THERE ANYTHING IN THERE YOU CAN'T REPLACE?

WHERE THE G☆#☆ AM I?
Welcome to ALBANY NEW YORK
3
LUGGAGE CAROUSEL 3

STEPH! STEPH! RAT WAS IN YOUR LOST LUGGAGE! HE SNUCK INSIDE BECAUSE HE DIDN'T WANT TO PAY FOR AIRLINE TICKETS! NOW HE'S LOST! WHAT ARE WE GONNA DO?!

WE SHOULD TRY TO GET HIM BACK, STEPH.
SHHHH. SAVOR THE MOMENT.

HELLO?
HI. THIS IS SOUTHWORSTERLY AIRLINES. WE'VE FOUND YOUR LUGGAGE WITH THE RAT INSIDE. HE'S UNHARMED, BUT A LITTLE ANGRY. WHERE WOULD YOU LIKE IT SENT?
1/19

YAKUTSK, SIBERIA
I'LL KILL HIM IF IT'S THE LAST THING I DO.

HI, PIG. I'M GONNA BE LEAVING THE STRIP FOR A WHILE. RAT JUST GOT BACK FROM SIBERIA AND I THINK HE'S A LITTLE UPSET WITH ME FOR SENDING HIM THERE.
OHH, HE JUST TALKS TOUGH. HE'LL GET OVER IT.

YEAH, YOU'RE PROBABLY RIGHT. BUT IT'S STILL A GOOD EXCUSE TO TAKE A VACATION.
OKAY, WELL IF YOU'RE REALLY GONNA GO, COME DOWN HERE AND GIMME A BIG HUG.
1/20

WOOSH WOOSH WOOSH
THWACK

IT'S NICE TO BE IN A STRIP SO FILLED WITH LOVE.

HEY, PIG. WHERE WERE YOU THIS MORNING?
I HAD TO GO WITH PIGITA TO THE DOCTOR'S OFFICE. SHE'S HAVING TROUBLE DRINKING MILK.
1/21

WHAT'D THE DOCTOR SAY?
HE SAID SHE HATES PEOPLE WHO ARE MISSING TOES.

THE TERM IS 'LACTOSE INTOLERANT.'
YEAH. AND TO ME, THAT'S RACIST.

STORY UPDATE:

Stephan Pastis is on the run from Rat, who is upset at Stephan for shipping him to Siberia. Today, Stephan's travels bring him to Kansas City, Missouri.

STORY UPDATE

Stephan Pastis has returned from Kansas City convinced that Rat's attack upon John Glynn has dissipated any anger Rat harbored toward him. Stephan now feels safe enough to enjoy a meal out with Pig and Goat.

STORY UPDATE:

Someone has taken a photo of a drunken Larry in a bar greeting a zebra with the crocodiles' sacred badonkadonk greeting, which involves one party rubbing his buttocks (badonkadonk) against that of the second party.

STORY UPDATE:

A drunken Larry was photographed rubbing his badonk-adonk against that of a zebra, which Larry then posted on Facebook. Larry returns to his croc fraternity in the hopes that the whole matter has quietly gone away.

LOOK AT THIS GUY WEARING SUNGLASSES INDOORS.
WHAT'S WRONG WITH THAT?

HE'S A TOOL. JUST WANTS TO SHOW US HOW AWESOME HE IS. MAKES ME WANT TO HIT HIM IN THE HEAD.
SHHHH. HE'LL HEAR YOU.

GOOD. LET HIM HEAR THIS...LIGHT IN HERE TOO BRIGHT FOR YOU, SUPERSTAR?

D'YOU SAY SOMETHING, PAL?
YEAH, I SAID SOME-THING. I SAID TAKE THIS, MR. TOO-COOL-FOR-THE-ROOM.

KONK

ARF
ARF
ARF
ARF
ARF
ARF

HE FELL ON A GUIDE DOG.
NOW WHAT'S A GUIDE DOG DOING THERE?
CHECK, PLEASE.

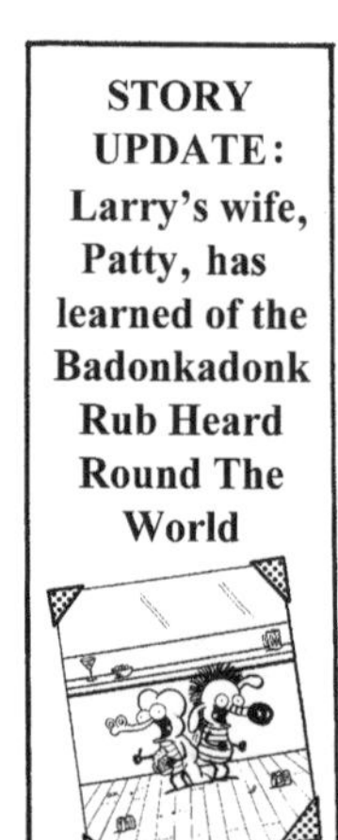

STORY UPDATE:

In exchange for Rat giving up his "Occupy Sesame Street" protest, PBS has agreed to make him host of "Mr. Rogers' Neighborhood."

MR. RAT'S NEIGHBORHOOD

HI, BOYS AND GIRLS...I THINK IT'S TIME FOR SOME MAKE-BELIEVE... OH, TROLLEY...COME TAKE US TO THE LAND OF MAKE-BELIEVE....

MR. RAT'S NEIGHBORHOOD

HI, BOYS AND GIRLS. THIS IS KING FRIDAY AND QUEEN SARA. KING FRIDAY IS USUALLY A HAPPY KING. BUT TODAY HE IS SAD. WHY? BECAUSE THE ARAB SPRING HAS THREATENED DESPOTIC MONARCHS EVERYWHERE.

MR. RAT'S NEIGHBORHOOD

HI, BOYS AND GIRLS. TODAY WE'RE GONNA LEARN ABOUT REVOLUTION, LIKE THE ONE JIHAD JERRY JUST PULLED OFF IN MR. RAT'S NEIGHBORHOOD.

AS YOU MAY NOTICE, I'M NOW DRESSED A LITTLE DIFFERENT. BUT DON'T WORRY, BOYS AND GIRLS. OTHER THAN THAT, EVERYTHING ELSE IN MR. RAT'S NEIGHBORHOOD WILL BE JUST LIKE IT ALWAYS WAS. ISN'T THAT RIGHT, MR. TROLLEY?

Die Imperialist Dogs

2/4

ALL I DO IS WORRY.
ABOUT WHAT?

THINGS THAT HAVE HAPPENED. THINGS THAT HAVEN'T HAPPENED. THINGS THAT MIGHT HAPPEN.
WHAT GOOD DOES THAT DO?

BECAUSE IF I DON'T WORRY, LIFE'S BAD STUFF WILL SNEAK UP ON ME. WORRYING IS MY WAY OF SAYING '@★#$% YOU, LIFE... YOU WON'T SURPRISE ME.'
BUT YOU BELIEVE LIFE IS BAD ANYWAY. SO WHY WORRY?

MAYBE YOU'RE RIGHT.
YEAH. SO CLOSE YOUR EYES AND RELAX.
RELAX.

CRACK

I'VE BEEN WAITING TEN YEARS TO DO THAT.
NEVER STOP WORRYING.

HEY, RAT, I HOPE YOU DON'T MIND, BUT I HAVE A COUPLE FRIENDS COMING OVER. THEY'RE ROADRUNNERS.
ROADRUNNERS ARE GREAT, DUDE. THEY'RE RIDICULOUSLY FAST. I'D LOVE TO JUST WATCH HOW THEY MOVE.

THAT'S DISAPPOINTING.

DO YOU EVER THINK THAT AS A SOCIETY WE'VE GROWN SOFT? THAT RATHER THAN RELY ON OUR GOD-GIVEN ABILITIES, WE NOW JUST RELY ON SOMEONE OR SOMETHING ELSE TO GIVE US A BOOST?
I DON'T THINK THAT'S TRUE. I THINK—
BEEP BEEP

SPARE A BUCK FOR TWO TIRED ROADRUNNERS?

THAT'S DISTURBING.
MONEY, PLEASE.

HEY, IF IT'S NOT MY GOOD FRIEND, JEFF THE CYCLIST! HOW ARE YOU, JEFF?
BETTER THAN YOU. AND THAT IS WHY I SHOW MY SUPERIORITY BY RIDING MY BIKE RIGHT IN FRONT OF YOUR CAR, INSTEAD OF IN THE BIKE LANE.

GOSH, JEFF, I WISH YOU WOULDN'T DO THAT BECAUSE—
EAT MY SPANDEX GREATNESS, FATTY McFAT FAT!!

AND THAT'S WHY I TRY TO RUN THEM OVER.
JEFF, YOU'RE ON MY BREAKFAST.
I STAMP OUT YOUR FATTENING FOOD AS A FAVOR TO YOU!!

I'VE SURE ENJOYED OUR DATE TONIGHT, PIGITA. BUT I WISH WE COULD DO SOMETHING THAT WAS EVEN MORE INTIMATE.
WHAT DO YOU HAVE IN MIND?

GROOMING FOR FLEAS. JUST LIKE MONKEYS.

SHE'S SO HARD TO READ.
2/9

HEY, PIG...I HEAR YOU'RE HAVING A BACKYARD BARBECUE...HOPE YOU DIDN'T INVITE A BUNCH OF LAZY FREELOADERS I DON'T LIKE.
NO, NO...I JUST INVITED GOAT AND ZEBRA. WHO ARE YOU WORRIED ABOUT?

ROADRUNNER EXPRESS
2/10

WE NEED TO START LOCKING THE GATE.

HEY THERE, GOAT. DID YOU ENJOY OUR BARBECUE YESTERDAY?
SURE DID. THANKS FOR INVITING ME.

YOU'RE WELCOME. AND HERE'S YOUR BILL.
BILL? YOU EXPECT ME TO PAY FOR A PARTY YOU INVITED ME TO?
2/11

NO. AND THAT'S WHY I'VE BROUGHT MY LAWYER.
PREPARE TO LOSE EVERYTHING.
I GIVE UP.
SUMMONS

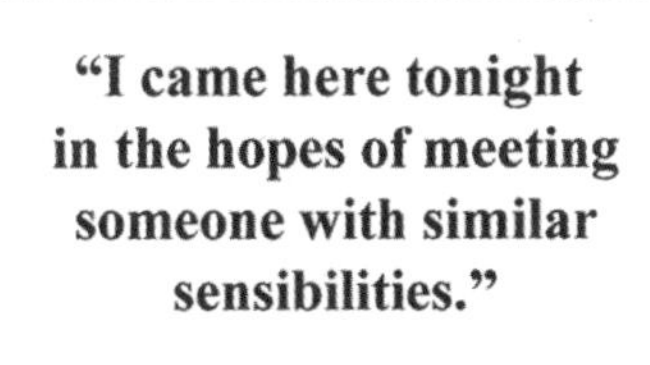

"Oh, silly me," said Elly. "All I've done is go on oafishly about myself. I'm sure you have much more erudite things to say."

HEY, JEFF THE CYCLIST. HOW ARE THINGS?
INTENSE. I HAVE TO PUT IN LONG HOURS TRAINING FOR MY NEXT RACE. MY WIFE AND KIDS DON'T SEEM TO UNDERSTAND.

I DIDN'T KNOW YOU HAD A WIFE AND KIDS. WHAT ARE THEIR NAMES?

2/13

YOU SHOULD SPEND MORE TIME WITH YOUR FAMILY, JEFF.
WAIT... I THINK ONE OF THEM IS A 'BETTY.'

DO YOU THINK THERE'S AN ELEMENT OF FRAUD IN MANY PROTESTS? THAT SOME PEOPLE RAIL AGAINST THE VERY THING THEY EXEMPLIFY?
I DON'T THINK THAT'S TRUE.

FIGHT LAZINESS
ROAD RUNNER EXPRESS
2/14

I'VE CHANGED MY MIND.
EXERCISE, PEOPLE!

WHAT DO YOU GOT THERE?
IT'S A LETTER SOME READER WROTE TO A NEWSPAPER ABOUT MY USE OF THE WORD 'ALRIGHT'... THE CORRECT TERM IS 'ALL RIGHT,' AND HE NEVER WANTS TO SEE IT WRITTEN AS 'ALRIGHT' IN THE STRIP AGAIN.
S. PASTIS

AND THIS GUY TOOK THE TIME TO WRITE AN ACTUAL LETTER TO THE NEWSPAPER SAYING THAT?
YEP.
S. PASTIS

IS THE POOR GUY ALRIGHT?
HEY, DON'T CRITICIZE HIM, ALRIGHT?
ALRIGHT, ALRIGHT, WHAT'S GOING ON HERE?
S. PASTIS

GUARD DUCK HAS A NEW MISSION. HE'S GONNA SNEAK UP ON NEGATIVE PEOPLE AND BITE THEIR BUTTOCKS.
SOUNDS LAME.

2/16

LET'S TRY TO REMAIN POSITIVE.

IF YOUR COUCH DUCK IS GONNA TERRORIZE US BY HIDING IN THE CUSHIONS, WE NEED TO START STARVING HIM OUT.

2/17
THERE'S ENOUGH FOOD IN HERE TO LAST THIRTY YEARS.

WE SHOULD VACUUM UNDER THE CUSHIONS NOW AND THEN.

OKAY, IF WE CAN'T STARVE OUT YOUR STUPID COUCH DUCK, WE CAN AT LEAST CLOSE HIS BANK ACCOUNTS. THAT WAY HE WON'T HAVE ANY CASH FOR NEW WEAPONS.

THERE'S SEVENTY THOUSAND DOLLARS IN LOOSE CHANGE DOWN HERE.
2/18

WE REALLY SHOULDA BEEN CHECKING UNDER THE CUSHIONS.

CAN I HELP YOU?
HI, ZEBRA, I'M VIRGINIA, THE VERTICALLY STRIPED ZEBRA... WE DATED FIVE YEARS AGO.

VIRGINIA! HOW HAVE YOU BEEN?
NOT GREAT. I'LL GET RIGHT TO THE POINT. WE HAVE A SON.

A SON? US? HOW DO YOU KNOW? I MEAN, HOW DO YOU KNOW HE'S MINE?
BECAUSE YOU'RE HORIZONTALLY STRIPED, AND I'M VERTICALLY STRIPED.

SO?
SO MEET OUR SON.
2/19

'PLAID.'

OH, GAWD.
TELL HIM HOW HARD IT'S BEEN, PLAID.
ACTUALLY, RIGHT NOW I'M IN STYLE.

GOSH, SON, I FEEL LIKE WE HAVE SO MUCH TIME TO MAKE UP FOR... WHAT WOULD YOU LIKE TO DO, PLAY BASEBALL, GO TO THE MOVIES, TRAVEL?
PLAY VIDEO GAMES.

WELL, THAT'S GREAT... AND WHAT ABOUT AFTER?
PLAY MORE VIDEO GAMES.

2/20
WELL, MAYBE IN YOUR TWENTIES WE CAN SPEND TIME TOGETHER.
I LOVE YOU, DAD, BUT LET'S TALK LESS.

HEY, SON, HOW WAS YOUR DAY?
GOOD. I KNOW YOU WANTED ME TO EASE UP ON THE VIDEO GAMES, SO I WENT OUTSIDE AND PLAYED WITH MY BLOW-DART GUN INSTEAD.

BLOW-DART GUN? IS THAT SAFE?
SURE. I DON'T AIM IT AT ANYBODY. I JUST TRY TO SHOOT IT OVER YOUR HEDGE.
THE HEDGE BEHIND THE HOUSE?
YEAH. WHY?
2/21

Pull teeng out of butt, Melvin!
Me no comfortable doing dat, Bob.

Whuh you doing, Bob?
Neighbahood no safe. Someone hunting crocs wid blow dart.
2/22

No one hunt us. We fierce. We top of food chain.
Gud point, Burt. Stand up. Yell someting.

NAILED THE LOUD ONE.
AHHHHHH! ME GOT BOO BOO! ME GOT BOO BOO!

Whuh we gonna do, Burt? Me keep geeting shot by blowdart assasseen. Buttocks een great pain.
We is pray to God of crocs. He save us.

2/23
Hullo, God of Crocs. Dis Bob and Burt. Someone shoot us. Peese make stop now.

Dis why me atheist, Burt.

Whuh you doing, Bob?
Me geet new God, Burt. Yours no save us.

Yours juss box.
He no juss box. He play moosic.
SPROING

Releegion very confusing, Bob.
My God so vengeful!
2/24

YO, ZEEBS, WHAT HAPPENED TO YOUR SON, 'PLAID'?
TURNS OUT HE WASN'T MY SON. I GUESS THERE ARE LOTS OF POTENTIAL ZEBRA DADS WITH STRIPES LIKE MINE, AND MY EX-GIRLFRIEND JUST PICKED THE WRONG ONE.

SOUNDS TO ME LIKE SOME WEASEL CARTOONIST DIDN'T KNOW WHERE TO GO WITH THE CHARACTER, SO HE JUST WIMPED OUT BY COMING UP WITH THAT STUPID EXPLANATION IN PANEL ONE.
2/25

THAT'S VERY INAPPROPRIATE.

THE WEASEL SPEAKS.
HEY! YOU TRY COMING UP WITH 365 IDEAS A YEAR!!

HEY, STEPHSTER, QUICK QUESTION.
WHAT IS IT? I'M TRYING TO DRAW.

JUST CURIOUS... WHAT'S THE HIGHEST HONOR IN ALL OF CARTOONING?
THE REUBEN AWARD. WHY?

THE REUBEN, HUH? I DON'T SUPPOSE YOU'VE EVER BEEN NOMINATED FOR THAT?
WHERE IS THIS GOING?

NOWHERE. HEY, JUST WONDERING. YOU HAVEN'T BY CHANCE BEEN NOMINATED THREE YEARS IN A ROW, HAVE YOU?
PLEASE... LEAVE.... RIGHT—

AND LOST MISERABLY EVERY SINGLE YEAR?!

I BUILT YOU A TROPHY SHELF. MIND IF I USE IT TO STORE GARBANZO BEANS?
THE PANTRY IS SOoooooo FULL.

LISTEN, STEPH, I KNOW THAT EVERY YEAR YOU'RE UP FOR CARTOONING'S HIGHEST AWARD, THE REUBEN, AND THAT EVERY YEAR YOU LOSE. SO NOW I FEEL BAD FOR BUILDING YOU THIS EMPTY TROPHY SHELF.
IS THAT SO?

YEAH, SO I BOUGHT YOU SOME DECORATIVE WOODEN LETTERS TO FILL THE SPACE. THEY'RE FUN TO REARRANGE IF YOU'RE EVER BORED.
WELL, I GUESS THAT'S PRETTY NICE OF YOU. THANKS.
ROLES

OH, LOOK. I'VE REARRANGED THEM.
TAKE THEM DOWN.
THAT DOES NOT LOOK LIKE A TROPHY.
LOSER

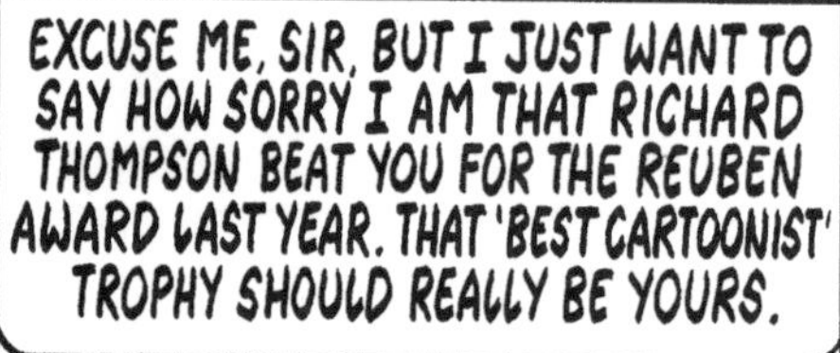
EXCUSE ME, SIR, BUT I JUST WANT TO SAY HOW SORRY I AM THAT RICHARD THOMPSON BEAT YOU FOR THE REUBEN AWARD LAST YEAR. THAT 'BEST CARTOONIST' TROPHY SHOULD REALLY BE YOURS.

WHOA WHOA WHOA...THAT'S NOT TRUE. RICHARD DESERVED THAT TROPHY. HIS 'CUL DE SAC' STRIP IS AWESOME. PLUS, RICHARD IS A KINDHEARTED, SWEET, HUMBLE GUY.

NOW I FEEL BAD FOR KNOCKING HIM UNCONSCIOUS.
TOLD YOU WE SHOULDN'T HAVE STOLEN THIS.

HEY, JEFF THE CYCLIST. WHAT ARE YOU HAVING FOR BREAK-FAST TODAY?
FIFTY GRAMS OF OATMEAL, ONE CUP OF BERRIES, AND A QUARTER CUP OF ALMONDS. IT'S ALL PART OF MY FITNESS REGIMEN.

THAT'S GREAT. HAVING A FITNESS REGIMEN IS IMPORTANT.
ESSENTIAL. AND WHAT IS YOURS?

I'VE STOPPED FRYING MY TWINKIES.

HEY, GOAT...I'D LIKE YOU TO MEET MY PALS, TIMMY AND TINA TURTLE. TIMMY DIED TEN YEARS AGO, BUT TINA STILL CARRIES HER DEAD HUSBAND'S SHELL ON HER BACK.
AWW. HOW SAD.

BEST TEN YEARS OF MARRIAGE WE'VE EVER HAD.

NEVER MIND.
SO, TIMMY...WHERE DO YOU WANT TO GO FOR DINNER? OH, YEAH...YOU DON'T HAVE A SAY.

HEY, ZEBRA, HAVE YOU MET MY FRIEND, TINA TURTLE? HER HUSBAND TIMMY DIED TEN YEARS AGO, SO ALL SHE DOES NOW IS COME HERE FOR BEER AND CARRY HIS SHELL ON HER BACK.

GEE, TINA, I'M SO SORRY...I GUESS HIS SHELL IS YOUR WAY OF HOLDING ON.

TO MY BEER. IT'S VERY HANDY.
FORGET IT.
MORE ICE, TINA TURTLE?
ICE

HEY, STEPH, I'M GETTING TAKE-OUT FROM THE DELI... WANT ANYTHING?
SURE. GET ME WHATEVER.

HI, I'D LIKE TO ORDER ONE B.L.T. AND A REUBEN SANDWICH FOR MY FRIEND....
OH, YOU'RE OUT OF REUBENS?

SO MY FRIEND CAN'T GET ONE? NO REUBEN AT ALL? NEVER? NEVER EVER? WHAT'S THAT YOU SAY? NOT EVEN IF HELL FREEZES OVER?

NOT EVEN IF WINGED PONIES FLY FROM MY REAR END WILL MY GOOD FRIEND STEPHAN PASTIS EVER EVER EVER GET A @#%@ REUBEN?!?

THEY'RE OUT.

PIGITA?
YES?

I HAVE SOMETHING TO CONFESS.
WHAT IS IT?

IT'S ABOUT US.
US??

I CHEATED ON YOU.

KSSSH
3/4

...BY LANDING ON 'MARVIN GARDENS' AND NOT PAYING YOU RENT.

OH.
YOU'RE A VERY INTENSE 'MONOPOLY' PLAYER.

WHAT'S WITH THE SIGN?
Me is support Newt Geengrich for Pressydent.
NEWT vote heem
NEWT

WHAT FOR?
Newts is fellow reptile. WE IS DOMINATE WORLD!
NEWT
3/5

NEWTS ARE AMPHIBIANS.

Politics so disillusioning.

GEET OUT of way, family... Me campayning 'gainst Geengrich.
SINCE WHEN DO YOU CARE ABOUT POLITICS?
NEWT BAD No U vote heem

Since amphibian try be Pressydent. Amphibians worst ting in world.
LARRY, THAT NEWT IS A HUMAN.

HAHAHAHAHAHA HAHAHAHAHAHA
NEWT BAD No U vote heem
3/6

And dat why we no let women vote, son.
WOMEN CAN VOTE, DAD.
LEMME SHOW YOU WHAT ELSE WOMEN CAN DO, LARRY.

WHY ARE YOU STILL CAMPAIGNING AGAINST NEWT GINGRICH, DAD?
Becuss amphibians beegest liars ever. One day dey has gills. One day dey has lungs. Dey like evil magicians.
No Newt
Newt is AMFIBIAN No u vote heem

DAD... STOP... THIS NEWT'S A HUMAN. I BROUGHT A PHOTO OF HIM. SEE... WHAT DO YOU THINK?
No Newt
Newt is AMFIBIAN No u vote heem

Dat amphibians learn grow human head.
No Newt
Newt is AMFIBIAN No u vote heem
3/7

NO.
Guy probblee laying eggs een swamp right now.
No Newt
Newt is AMFIBIAN No u vote heem

NEWT GINGRICH PRESS CONFERENCE
....AND THAT'S WHAT I THINK OF INDIVIDUAL MANDATES. I HAVE TIME FOR ONE MORE QUESTION, FOLKS....

WHERE YOU LAY YOUR EGGS, AMPHIBIAN ??
GUY NO Human. Ees AmFibiAN
No Newt
No truss AmFibian
3/8

WHAT THE HELL IS GOING ON?
SHOW US YOU GILLS!
SHOW US YOU WEBBED FEET!

Dear Mitts Romnee, Newt guy you running against no is human. He evil amfibian.
Newt badd

How you prove?
Newt badd
3/9

At next deebate, hold guy underwater, see if can breathe.
Newt badd

P.S. For dis tip, me expekt be made Vice-Pressydent.
Newt baddd

HOW YOU GONNA FINISH THE NEWT SERIES? IT'S DECEMBER WHEN YOU'RE WRITING THIS AND YOU HAVE NO IDEA WHERE GINGRICH'S CAMPAIGN WILL BE WHEN THE SERIES RUNS.
3/10

CUT OUT IF WRONG
NO IDEA ??... NEWT DROPPED OUT!!... HAHAHAHAHAHAHAHA
No Newt

CUT OUT IF WRONG
NO IDEA?...NEWT EES NOMINEE!!... AHHHHHHHHHHHHH
No Newt

YOU SLIMY CHEAT.
NO IDEA? JON HUNTSMAN WON EVERYTING!!
OKAY, LET'S NOT GET SILLY.
No Newt

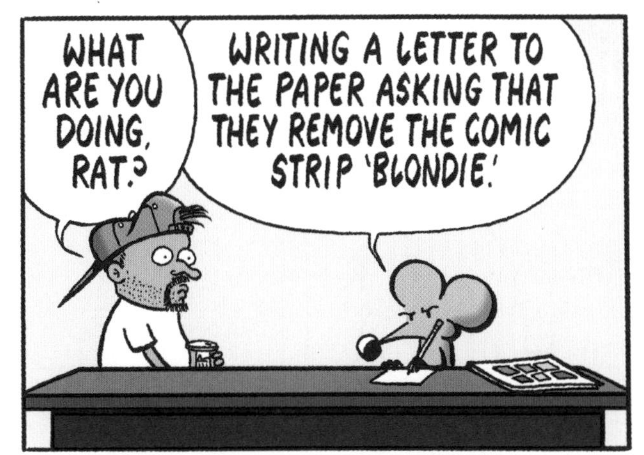
WHAT ARE YOU DOING, RAT?
WRITING A LETTER TO THE PAPER ASKING THAT THEY REMOVE THE COMIC STRIP 'BLONDIE.'

'BLONDIE'? WHAT'S WRONG WITH 'BLONDIE'?
LOOK AT HER.

WHAT?... IT'S BLONDIE.
LOOK AT HER RIGHT HAND.

3/11

I DON'T—
SHE'S FLASHING GANG SIGNS!!

THEY SHOULD REMOVE **YOU** FROM THE PAPER.
YO, BLONDIE! *KIDS* READ THIS SECTION!!

WHO'S YOUR FAVORITE PAINTER?
MAYBE VAN GOGH. WHY?

BECAUSE MINE IS RUBENS. BUT I'M NOT SURE OF HIS FIRST NAME.
I THINK IT'S PETER PAUL RUBENS.
3/12

REALLY? 'CAUSE I THOUGHT IT WAS "MY-CARTOONING'S-SO-CRAPPY-I-WON'T-BE-WINNING-A-LOT-OF" RUBENS.

YOU SEEM TO DISAGREE.

YO, TOON BOY, WHATCHA WRITING?
JUST A 'PEARLS' STRIP THAT I—
BLAM
BLAM
BLAM

WHAT THE @☆#☆ WAS THAT?
IT'S 'BEETLE BAILEY' CREATOR MORT WALKER TRYING TO TAKE US OUT! IT'S A RE-KINDLING OF THE EAST COAST/WEST COAST CARTOONISTS' WAR! EVERYONE GRAB AN UZI!!
3/13

CARTOONISTS ARE AN ODD BUNCH.

HEY, STEPH, CAN I ASK WHY WE'RE PUTTING MATTRESSES IN FRONT OF THE WINDOW?
IT'S A RE-KINDLING OF THE EAST COAST/WEST COAST CARTOONISTS' WAR. IT FLARES UP EVERY FEW YEARS.
3/14

BUT YOU GUYS SHOULD BE DRAWING FUNNY DOODLES AND—
BLAM
BLAM
BLAM

SORRY... I HAD TO CAP ANDY CAPP.
LOOK... HE'S SO DRUNK HE DIDN'T FEEL IT.

LISTEN, PIG, THIS EAST COAST/WEST COAST CARTOONISTS' WAR IS GONNA GET UGLY, BUT DON'T WORRY, 'CAUSE WE HAVE THE ULTIMATE BAD@## ON OUR SIDE, AND THAT'S GUARD DUCK.

GEE, STEPH..I DUNNO..THE POOR GUY'S BEEN SO HIGH-STRUNG LATELY THAT I SENT HIM ON A RETREAT.
RETREAT? TO WHERE?

OHMMMMMMMMMM
TIBETAN PEACE, LOVE AND MEDITATION CENTER

STEPH, WHAT THE G#☆ IS THIS EAST COAST/WEST COAST CARTOONISTS' FEUD?
SYNDICATION'S A ROUGH BUSINESS, GOAT, SO EVERY FEW YEARS, CARTOONISTS FROM THE EAST COAST FIGHT ALONGSIDE THEIR CHARACTERS AGAINST ALL OF US WEST COAST GUYS AND ALL OF OUR CHARACTERS.
ZING

BUT WE DON'T HAVE GUARD DUCK RIGHT NOW...WHAT WEST COAST CHARACTERS DO WE HAVE THAT CAN MAKE UP FOR THAT?

SHOOT ME NOW.

THE CARTOONISTS' WAR
RAT! RAT! THAT CUTE L'IL DOG AND CAT FROM 'MUTTS' BROKE IN AND KIDNAPPED STEPHAN AT KNIFEPOINT! THEY WANT $10,000 TO GIVE HIM BACK!
NEVER

YOU DON'T WANT TO PAY?
I DON'T WANT STEPHAN BACK.

POOR STEPHAN.
NOW IF THEY WANT CASH TO KEEP HIM, I'LL TALK.

WHAT ARE YOU DOING WITH A HAMMER?
Ees genetic adaptation. Ees better equip us keel zeeba.

WHAT ARE YOU TALKING ABOUT?
Bob here esspert. We hire heem essplain whole ting. He reely smart. Geev us superior knowledge.

YEAH, WELL, BOB'S INCORRECT. A GENETIC ADAPTATION TAKES PLACE OVER MILLIONS OF YEARS. PLUS, IT'S A MODIFICATION OF THE ANIMAL'S D.N.A., AND IT FUNDAMENTALLY CHANGES ITS INNATE ABILITY TO SURVIVE.

3/18

CRACK

Me fundamentally change Bob.

THE CARTOONISTS' WAR

STORY UPDATE: Stephan Pastis has been taken hostage by the evil East Coast geniuses, Earl and Mooch

SOMETIMES I WONDER IF I HAVE FAITH IN ANYTHING, BUT I'M NOT SURE I KNOW WHAT FAITH IS.
IT'S BELIEVING IN SOMETHING...TRUSTING AND RELYING ON IT WITHOUT QUESTION. IS THERE SOMETHING IN YOUR LIFE THAT MEETS THAT STANDARD?

CHEESE.

MAYBE I DIDN'T DEFINE THAT WELL.
IF YOU'LL EXCUSE ME, I NEED TO BUILD A CHURCH.

I GOT TWO HUNDRED COMPLAINTS ABOUT THIS FEBRUARY 8TH STRIP WHERE YOU SAY YOU TRY TO RUN OVER PEOPLE LIKE JEFF, THE ANNOYING CYCLIST.
BUT I'M JUST A CARTOON CHARAC-TER.

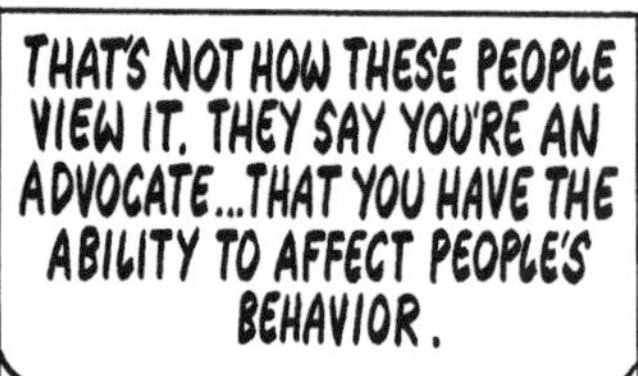
THAT'S NOT HOW THESE PEOPLE VIEW IT. THEY SAY YOU'RE AN ADVOCATE...THAT YOU HAVE THE ABILITY TO AFFECT PEOPLE'S BEHAVIOR.

BREAK STEPHAN'S FINGERS!! BREAK STEPHAN'S FINGERS!!

HAVING FUN?
WHAT'S TAKING THESE PEOPLE SO LONG?

Dear Girls,
I am not smart. I'm fat. I'm poor. And I'm ugly.

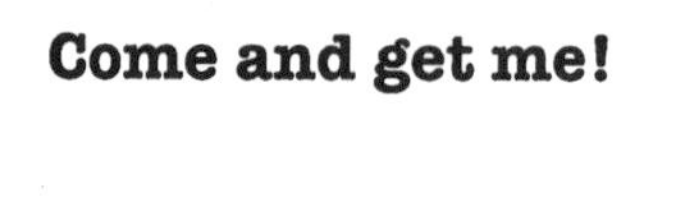
Come and get me!

YOUR SINGLES AD LEAVES SOMETHING TO BE DESIRED.

JOE'S
TERRACE
BURGERS

ORDER
FOOD
HERE

CAN I HELP YOU?
YEAH...WHAT DO I WANT...HMMMM...

MAYBE A CHEESEBURGER?... NO, NO.... JUST PLAIN.... NO, NO.... CHEESE.
FOR HERE OR TO GO?
FOR HERE OR TO GO...HMMM..
3/25

DUDE...YOU HAD THAT ENTIRE G#☆#G#☆ LINE TO DECIDE ALL THIS AND YOU WAIT 'TIL *NOW* TO DECIDE?!
OUT OF MY FACE, PAL.

JOE'S
TERRACE
BURGERS
HURL
AAHHHHH

MAKE HIS TO GO.

WHERE'S RAT TODAY?
SHOPPING. HE'S LOOKING FOR SOMETHING THAT LETS HIM SIT WHEREVER HE WANTS YET ALWAYS HAVE A BEER HANDY.
3/26

SQUEAK SQUEAK SQUEAK SQUEAK SQUEAK

GOTTA LOVE THE BABY STORE.

I CAN'T BELIEVE IT. YOU'RE REALLY GOING TO GO AROUND IN A BABY WALKER?
YUP. I JUST ROLL AROUND AND DRINK BEER. MY GOAL IS TO NEVER HAVE TO GET UP TO DO ANYTHING AGAIN.

WELL, YOU'LL OBVIOUSLY HAVE TO GET UP TO DO SOME THINGS.

I GOT WHAT YOU ASKED ME TO GET, RAT.
I'M GOING NOW.
NO, NO. *I'M* GOING NOW.
DIAPERS
3/27

HOW'S IT GOING, SIR?
NOT GOOD, L'IL GUARD DUCK. I'M HAVING FRIENDS OVER FOR LUNCH AND I CAN'T GET THE MAYONNAISE LID LOOSE.
MAYO

3/28
BLAM!!

IT'S LOOSE NOW, SIR.
WELL, NOW, THAT'S A HANDY-DANDY KITCHEN DEVICE.

IF THE CHOICE WAS YOURS, HOW WOULD YOU CHOOSE TO DIE?
I DON'T KNOW... I GUESS RIGHT HERE DRAWING AT MY DRAWING TABLE.
3/29

BY NATURAL CAUSES.
FELT PRETTY NATURAL TO ME.

HEY, NEIGHBOR MELANIE! HOW ARE THINGS? HOW'S YOUR HUSBAND?
TERRIFIC, PIG! WE'VE BEEN GETTING ALONG GREAT EVER SINCE WE DECIDED TO COMMUNICATE BETTER AND BE MORE OPEN WITH EACH OTHER.
3/30

WHAT ARE YOU TWO YAPPING ABOUT?
OH, SORRY, RAT. THIS IS MELANIE. SHE AND HER HUSBAND NOW HAVE AN OPEN MARRIAGE.

WELL, NOW, HER MOOD SURE CHANGED FAST.

WHAT DO YOU DREAM OF BEING WHEN YOU'RE OLDER?

OH, A TOY SHOP OWNER! I'D HAVE ALL THE TOYS I EVER WANTED FOR FREE!!
C
A B
3/31

TOY SHOP OWNERS DON'T GET TOYS FOR FREE. THEY PAY FOR THEM.
C
A B

LIFE IS CRUEL.

Zeeba neighba....

WHAT?
Dere no barrier. No bush. No fence. Nutting stop us keel you. Dis beeg moment me wait for.

FIST BUMP

CHEST BUMP

Speech! Speech!
Okay...Uh...Good knowing you...Me hate you face... Die.

AARGHHH
4/1

THWACK
THWACK

Guy protected by force field, Bob.
Curse you, techmology.

HELLO, RAT. MAY I PLEASE HAVE SOME COFFEE?
SURE, PIG. LET ME HAND YOU SOME.....

COFFEE...
4/2

IT WORKED! IT WORKED!
FIRST 3D COMIC EVER.
GIVE ME MY COFFEE BACK.

HEY, RAT, MY FRIEND TIMMY IS COMING OVER TODAY TO HELP ME DIG A DITCH. HE'S REALLY SHORT AND HAS A BEARD.
IS THAT HIM?

WHAT HAPPENED?
I THOUGHT IT WAS A LEPRECHAUN HIDING ITS POT OF GOLD.
4/3

HE REALLY SHOULDN'T WEAR GREEN.
HEY, I DID GET A WALLET.

EXCUSE ME, SIR, BUT YOUR CAT SNUFFLES WOULD LIKE YOU TO KNOW HOW UPSET HE IS THAT ANOTHER CAT FROM THE NEIGHBORHOOD HAS BEEN USING HIS LITTERBOX.
YEAH, WELL I'M TAKING CARE OF MY NEIGHBOR'S CAT, BOOTSIES, SO HE'S JUST GONNA HAVE TO LEARN TO SHARE FOR A WHILE.
4/4

KABOOM

TOLD YOU WE SHOULDN'T HAVE MINED THE LITTERBOX.

WHAT ARE YOU DOING, RAT?
STUDYING HOW TO BE A KNIGHT FROM THE MIDDLE AGES. THESE GUYS HATED TALKING TO THE IDIOTS AROUND THEM SO MUCH THAT THEY HID INSIDE A SUIT OF METAL.
4/5

WHAT ARE YOU TALKING ABOUT? THAT'S NOT WHY KNIGHTS WORE ARMOR. THEY WORE IT BECAUSE——

THAT'S RATHER RUDE.
NUTS. I CAN STILL HEAR YE.

WHERE'S RAT TODAY?
HE HAS TO SPEND EASTER WITH HIS FAMILY.

I THOUGHT HE HATED SPENDING HOLIDAYS WITH HIS FAMILY.
HE DOES, BUT HE SAYS HE HAS A WAY OF DEALING WITH IT NOW.
4/6

WE KNOW YOU'RE IN THERE.

WHY DO PEOPLE HATE EACH OTHER OVER RACIAL AND RELIGIOUS AND POLITICAL DIFFERENCES WHEN IT'S SO OBVIOUS THAT FUNDAMENTALLY THERE ARE ONLY TWO KINDS OF PEOPLE?
WHICH ARE WHAT?

GOOD PEOPLE AND PEOPLE WHO USE THE WORD 'WHOM'.
4/7

TO WHOM ARE YOU REFERRING?
WHOMER, REPENT!
LOVE THE WHO, HATE THE WHOMER

WHAT DO YOU HAVE THERE, PIG?
SOME OF MY PEZ COLLECTION.

I DIDN'T KNOW YOU COLLECTED PEZ.
OH, YEAH. IT'S GREAT TRYING TO COLLECT THE BEST ONES.

WHAT DO YOU LOOK FOR?
THE ONES WITH THE MOST 'PEZNESS.'

WHAT'S THAT?
PROPER HEAD-TO-BODY RATIO, COLOR, AND MOST OF ALL, RARITY.

AND WHICH ONES HAVE ALL THAT?
PEZNESS? GOSH, WELL, MY YODA, THE TIN MAN, MY WILLIAM SHATNER. BUT THE BEST OF THE BEST IS THE ONE OF THE STAND-UP COMIC MARGARET CHO. ALMOST NO ONE HAS IT.

THAT ONE'S GOOD?
GOOD?

THERE'S NOooo PEZNESS LIKE CHO PEZNESS!

I MADE IT USING HIS ACTUAL HEAD.
PEZ
4/8

GUNS DON'T COME FROM BATHROOMS, LARRY. SOMEONE PUT THAT IN THERE FOR MICHAEL TO FIND LATER... SO WHAT DOES THAT MEAN? YOU SENT BOB TO THE RESTAURANT AND HAVE NO GUN WAITING FOR HIM IN THE BATHROOM?

SHUT MOUF, WOOMUN! ME HAS BACKUP PLAN!!

Whuh you mean, beat Zeeba wid toilet paper roll.?

UPDATE:
Bob and Larry have set up a "Godfather"-inspired hit on Zebra at a restaurant. But no gun was waiting for Bob in the bathroom. Instead, his only available weapon is toilet paper.

STORY UPDATE

Unable to pull off the "Godfather"-style hit on Zebra with extra-soft toilet paper, the crocs send Bob out for a better weapon... regular toilet paper.

STORY UPDATE

Larry and Bob have bought the hardest toilet paper they can find to bash Zebra over the head while he is on a date at a restaurant.

Danny Donkey hated people.
It's true.

So Danny Donkey bought a treehouse at the top of a very tall tree.

"You should invite the entire neighborhood to a housewarming party," said Danny's perky real estate agent. "Then you'll have good relationships with all your neighbors."

So Danny Donkey invited all his neighbors to a house-warming party.

Which went well until he ran out of champagne.
You ran out of champagne, dude.
Yeah. You call this a party?

So Danny excused himself to buy more champagne.
More bubbly on the way.

And chopped down the tree.
Ahhh
No
Scream
Timb-e-e-e-r

"Now I have good relationships with all my neighbors," exclaimed Danny Donkey.

'SO REMEMBER, KIDS, IT'S NOT GOOD FENCES THAT MAKE GOOD NEIGHBORS. IT'S DECEASED NEIGHBORS THAT MAKE GOOD NEIGHBORS.'
I GIVE UP.
ARE ALL THESE PEOPLE WITH X's FOR EYES JUST NAPPING?

WHAT ARE YOU DOING, PIG?
JUST GETTING OUTSIDE FOR A CHANGE...ENJOYING NATURE...IT'S SO PEACEFUL...SO HARMONIOUS... THE BIRDS, THE FISH, THE INSECTS...

ALL OF WHOM ARE TRYING TO KILL EACH OTHER.

LET'S NEVER LEAVE THE LIVING ROOM AGAIN.
BEER
4/16

WITH ALL THESE NEW TECHNOLOGIES COMING OUT EVERY DAY, DOESN'T IT SOMETIMES FEEL LIKE WE'RE LIVING IN AN AGE OF MIRACLES?
TIMES DISPATCH

OH, YEAH. LIKE HOW WHEN YOU PULL OUT A KLEENEX, THE NEXT ONE MIRACULOUSLY APPEARS?

NO.
HOW DO THEY *DO* IT?
4/17

HEY, GOAT, SORRY THAT YESTERDAY I WAS SO AMAZED AT HOW WHEN YOU PULL A KLEENEX OUT OF THE BOX, THE NEXT ONE AUTOMATICALLY APPEARS. RAT EXPLAINED TO ME HOW THEY DO IT.
THAT'S OKAY, PIG... AT LEAST NOW YOU UNDERSTAND.

YEAH. BUT HOW DO THEY GET THAT LITTLE MAN IN THERE WHO RADIOS BACK TO KLEENEX HEADQUARTERS?

HE'S VERY SMALL.
DO YOU NEED FOOD?!
CHECK, PLEASE.
4/18

WHAT ARE YOU DOING, PIG?
TRYING TO FIND KLEENEX BOB. HE'S THE LITTLE MAN IN THE KLEENEX BOX WHO RADIOS BACK TO HEADQUARTERS WHENEVER YOU TAKE OUT A KLEENEX.

WHAT ARE YOU TALKING ABOUT?
IT'S HOW KLEENEX HEADQUARTERS KNOWS TO POP THE NEXT KLEENEX OUT OF THE BOX! HE'S A CRITICAL PART OF THE OPERATION! AND I CAN'T FIND HIM ANYWHERE! BECAUSE HE'S LOST! LOST!
4/19

I THINK I'LL SHOW MYSELF OUT.
SHHH. SENDING IN A SEARCH PARTY.

HEY, RAT.... HOW COME PIG WASN'T AT THE DINER THIS MORNING?
HE HAS GOOSEBUMPS.

SINCE WHEN DO GOOSEBUMPS KEEP SOMEONE FROM GOING OUT FOR COFFEE?
NEXT TIME PAY YOUR DEBTS.
NEVER MIND.
LOOK...IT'S A GOOSEKICKTOTHE-GROIN.
4/20

LOOK AT ALL THIS E-MAIL. I'VE GOT HUNDREDS I HAVEN'T EVEN READ.
HOW DO YOU RESPOND TO ALL THOSE?

WELL, ONE LITTLE SHORTCUT I'VE LEARNED IS TO FIRST CLICK THE 'SELECT ALL' FEATURE.
THEN WHAT?

[Delete]
4/21

IT'S A BIG TIME-SAVER.

OH, YEAH. I TOLD 'EM, "YOU DON'T MESS WITH THE COLOR IN *MY* STRIP. I'M STEPHAN PASTIS, DARN IT." I THINK THAT REALLY INTIMIDATED THEM.

4/22

I HATE EVERYBODY. I HATE EVERYTHING.
YOU KNOW, IF YOU'RE SO UNHAPPY, YOU SHOULD THINK ABOUT MOVING ABROAD.

4/23

DIDN'T HELP.

Hullo zeeba neighba. Leesten. You got long arms? Me drop keys through grate.
OH, YOU MEAN THE SEWER GRATE?

Barbeecue.
EET Zeebas
4/24

Dat guy never helpful.
EET Zeebas

I JUST READ THOMAS MANN'S NOVEL 'DEATH IN VENICE.'
GREAT. THAT'S A REAL CLASSIC.

OH, AND I CAN SEE WHY. MAN GOES TO VENICE. MAN DIES.

A CLASSIC!!!
4/25

MAYBE GREAT LITERATURE ISN'T YOUR THING.
SO IS 'CLASSIC' CODE FOR BORING AND SUCKY?

HEY, RAT...I'D LIKE YOU TO MEET OUR NEWEST CHARACTER, MIKEY THE MOLE.
THAT'S IT?...HE'S JUST A MOLE? NO WEIRD FREAKISH TRAIT LIKE ALL OUR OTHER CHARACTERS?

FOOSHHH

HE DOES SPONTANEOUSLY COMBUST.
IT'S ALWAYS SOMETHING.
FEEL FREE TO ROAST MARSH-MALLOWS.
4/26

HEY, RAT, I COULDN'T HELP BUT NOTICE YOU'RE NOT EATING YOUR SOUP THE RIGHT WAY.... WHEN YOU DIP THE SPOON, YOU'RE SUPPOSED TO MOVE IT AWAY FROM YOU, NOT TOWARD YOU.

LIKE THAT?
JAB
JAB
JAB
4/27

NOT QUITE.
SHOULD I TRY AGAIN, MISS MANNERS?

WHAT ARE YOU DOING, PIG?
PLAYING PING PONG WITH RAT.

BUT HE'S JUST SMASHING THE BALL INTO YOUR FACE.
YEAH. RAT SAYS THE 'PING' IS WHEN YOU HIT IT WITH THE PADDLE, BUT THE 'PONG' IS WHEN YOU SMASH SOMEONE'S FACE. OTHERWISE, HE SAYS IT'D BE CALLED 'PING PING.'
4/28

THAT IS NOT HOW YOU PLAY—
MAY I ONE DAY BE A PINGER?
A PONGER BE A PINGER? NOW I HAVE TO PADDLE YOU FOR ASKING.

Hullooo, zeeba neighba, leesten... Crocs buy eendustrial strengf trash compakker.
WHAT FOR?
4/29

Shove you eenside. Crush you like Hefty bag.

DO YOU THINK THAT CAN CRUSH AN ANIMAL MY SIZE?

Do me tink? Me know. Me and Burt be like professional scientist. Did many test.
WHERE'S BURT?

He scream a lot for professional scientist.

DID YOU HEAR THAT THE GRIM REAPER GUY IS MOVING BACK INTO THE HOUSE NEXT DOOR TO YOU? I GUESS HE AND MRS. DEATH WERE SEPARATED FOR A WHILE.
YEAH, I SURE MISSED MR. DEATH. I'M EVEN MAKING A SIGN ON BEHALF OF THE NEIGHBORHOOD WELCOMING HIM BACK.

THIS TOWN WELCOMES DEATH

MAYBE WE COULD RE-WORD THAT.
HOW 'BOUT THIS?
EAGERLY AWAITING DEATH
4/30

HEY THERE, PIG. JUST WANTED TO SAY THANKS FOR BEING SO NICE AND WELCOMING ME BACK TO THE NEIGHBORHOOD.
IT'S MY PLEASURE, MR. DEATH. HEY, HOW COME YOU'RE NOT WEARING THE GIFT I GOT YOU? I BOUGHT IT ON MY LAST VACATION.

OH, THAT?... WELL...I...
OH, C'MON, MR. DEATH. YOU'RE REALLY GONNA HURT MY FEELINGS.

HAPPY?
YOU LOOK SOOOO CUTE.
5/1

LOOK AT THAT GUY HOLDING HIS CELL PHONE SO CLOSE TO HIS HEAD. DO YOU THINK IT'S TRUE THAT THOSE THINGS CAN BE DANGEROUS TO YOUR HEALTH?
YAP YAP YAP YAP YAP YAP YAP YAP YAP YAP

CRACK

SOMETIMES.
5/2

HEY, PIG, I WANT YOU TO MEET ONE OF THE BEST ENTERTAINMENT LAWYERS IN HOLLYWOOD.... I'M SELLING A 'PEARLS' MOVIE SCRIPT AND HE'S GONNA HELP ME.
HI. I'M LES ABELL.

OHH, DON'T SAY THAT. I BET IF YOU TRY A LITTLE HARDER, ONE DAY YOU'LL BE JUST AS GOOD AS ALL THE OTHER LAWYERS.
5/3

WHAT THE @☆#@ IS HE TALKING ABOUT?
PIG... HE'S *LES ABELL*.
WELL, DON'T SAY IT IN FRONT OF HIM.

'PROMOTE PEACE'... 'CO-EXIST'... 'SAVE THE PLANET'... WHY DO PEOPLE ALWAYS TELL ME WHAT TO DO ON THEIR BUMPER STICKERS?

I DON'T KNOW. WHY DOES IT MATTER?
BECAUSE IT BOTHERS ME. SO I'VE CREATED MY OWN.
5/4

Stop telling me what to do on your bumper stickers.

I THINK IT HURTS YOUR CASE THAT IT'S ON A BUMPER STICKER.
HEY. STOP TELLING ME WHAT TO DO.

WHAT'S THE KEY TO BEING HAPPY?
I THINK IT'S LEARNING TO LIVE IN THE MOMENT.

WHICH MOMENT? BECAUSE MANY OF MINE ARE CRAPPY.
5/5

THIS MOMENT.
THIS MOMENT? OH, HOW BORING.

HEY, NEIGHBOR WILLY! WANT TO FLY TO MARS?
CAN'T. HAVE TO STUDY.
Hello, My Name is Pig
Rockitt Shipp
5/6

WHY?
I NEED A 4.6 G.P.A.
WHAT FOR?
Hello, My Name is Pig
Rockitt Shipp

TO GET INTO A TOP-TIER, IVY LEAGUE SCHOOL.

WHERE, IF I WORK REALLY HARD, I CAN GET A DEGREE AND THEN A SIX-FIGURE JOB.

WHERE, IF I WORK EVEN HARDER, I CAN MAKE A LOT OF MONEY FOR MANY YEARS.

WHICH, IF EVERY-THING GOES RIGHT, WILL ALLOW ME TO RETIRE COMFORTABLY AT 65.

THEN WHAT?
THEN MAYBE I'LL HAVE A COUPLE YEARS LEFT BEFORE I DIE.
Hello, My Name is Pig
Rockitt Shipp

Hello, My Name is Pig
Rockitt Shipp

WILLY
Rockitt Shipp

WELL, GOAT, I'M OFF... I JOINED 'TOASTMASTERS INTERNATIONAL' AND HAVE MY FIRST MEETING.
GOOD FOR YOU, PIG. ARE YOU GOING TO IMPROVE YOUR PUBLIC SPEAKING SKILLS?

5/7

IT APPEARS THERE'S BEEN A MISUNDERSTANDING.

WHAT'S THE MATTER WITH YOU, PIG?
IT'S MY NEIGHBOR, JUAN. HE'S SO RUDE TO PEOPLE, BUT I DON'T THINK HE REALIZES IT.

WELL, IT CAN BE PAINFUL FOR SOME PEOPLE TO SEE THEMSELVES AS THEY TRULY ARE.
SO IT ACHES JUAN TO KNOW JUAN?
5/8

SURELY, YOU CAN DO BETTER.

HEY, PIGITA... MY NEIGHBORS BOB AND BETTY ASKED IF WE'D BE INTERESTED IN DOING SOMETHING WITH THEM.

I DON'T KNOW ANYTHING ABOUT THEM.
WELL, FOR ONE THING, THEY'RE SWINGERS.
5/9

SHE DOESN'T APPROVE OF YOUR LIFESTYLE.

MY NEIGHBOR, MR. DEATH, STARTED A SHOE REPAIR BUSINESS. IT'S PRETTY CONVENIENT. HE PICKS UP THE WORN-OUT SHOES RIGHT FROM THE CUSTOMERS' HOMES.
HOW'S THAT GOING?

NOT SO WELL.
WHY NOT?

I'VE COME FOR YOUR SOLE.
5/10

SORRY I'M LATE, GOAT. THERE WAS SOME CONSTRUCTION, SO I HAD TO WALK A DIFFERENT WAY.
THAT'S OKAY. HEY, I'D LIKE YOU TO MEET MY FRIEND, CHRIS...CHRIS, THIS IS PIG.
PIG, HUH? WHAT DO YOU GO BY?

THE CHEESE STORE AND THE BAKERY.
5/11

A NAME, PIG...HE'S LOOKING FOR A NAME.
OH, I THINK IT'S 'LOU'S CHEESE STORE.' THEY HAVE VERY GOOD CHEESE.
NEVER MIND.

EXCUSE ME, SIR, BUT WOULD YOU LIKE TO SUPPORT OUR CAUSE? MAYBE SIGN SOME OF OUR PETITIONS?
I'M SORRY. I'M NOT VERY POLITICAL.
SUPPORT

OH, PLEASE, SIR...WE'VE BEEN OUT HERE IN THE HOT SUN ALL DAY. COULD YOU AT LEAST JUST WEAR ONE OF OUR SHIRTS OR SOMETHING?
ALRIGHT, ALRIGHT, FINE.
SUPPORT
5/12

THIS IS AWKWARD.
PRO LIFE

BOB! BOB! Guess whuh me see.
Whuh?

Dead deer. On highway. Stoopid tings try run across. Geet hit.
Dead deer taste gud.

Me know dat, Bob. So go steal beegest truck possible. We zoom down highway. Run over everyting.

5/13

How 'bout YOU go run across highway, Bob?
GIMME BACK THE CART, PAL.
Peese no hit me, Man-Een-Funny-Pants.

Okay, woomun, leesten..Crocs geet wheels. Run over deer. Eet.
THAT'S A GOLF CART, LARRY. IT'S NOT GONNA RUN OVER ANYTHING.
Whoa whoa whoa, Ms. Larry. Dat no true.

Me run over beetle.
5/14

Next time me do talking, Bob.
Hey, whuh you know...leetle guy still alive.

EXCUSE ME, GOAT, BUT IS THAT THE 'NEW YORK TIMES' YOU'RE PERUSING?
YES. WHY?

FOOOSH
5/15

NO COMICS SECTION.
SUPPORT OUR OWN, SIR.

IS THAT THE 'WALL STREET JOURNAL'?
WHOA WHOA WHOA.. YESTERDAY, YOU HAD GUARD DUCK TORCH MY 'NEW YORK TIMES' WITH A FLAME THROWER BECAUSE IT DIDN'T HAVE COMICS. IS THAT WHY YOU'RE ASKING?

NO, NO, NO. JUST BECAUSE A NEWSPAPER DOESN'T HAVE A COMICS SECTION IS NO REASON TO BURN IT WITH A FLAME THROWER.
GREAT. THANKS.

FIRE IN THE HOLE!!
5/16

HAND GRENADES ARE NOT AN IMPROVEMENT.
THEN READ A PAPER WITH COMICS, TRAITOR.
BE LOYAL TO THE ART FORM, SIR.

WHAT ARE YOU READING?
THIS COMEDIAN'S AUTOBIOGRAPHY. HE TALKS A LOT ABOUT GROWING UP AND HOW HIS PARENTS MESSED HIM UP.

INTERESTING. SO HIS PARENTS MESSED HIM UP, HUH? I DON'T SUPPOSE THAT'S A LITTLE BIT LIKE THE STORY OF, UHH....

EVERY OTHER PERSON ON THE PLANET??
5/17

I THINK I KNOW WHY YOUR BLOOD PRESSURE IS SO HIGH.
BECAUSE THERE ARE SO MANY MORONS?

2:52 Sipped coffee.

WHAT ARE YOU DOING?
RECORDING MY EVERY ACTION SO FUTURE BIOGRAPHERS WILL HAVE AN ACCURATE RECORD OF MY EVERY MOVE.

DON'T YOU THINK IT'S A LITTLE ARROGANT TO ASSUME THAT ONE DAY PEOPLE WILL WANT TO CHRONICLE YOUR LIFE?
5/18

2:53 Silenced doubters.

HIYA, PIG...MEET MISTER MUFFATONI, THE PUPPET ON A STICK WHO MAKES SNAP JUDGMENTS ABOUT WHO HE LIKES.
SNAP JUDGMENTS MEANING QUICK?

WHAP
5/19

I'D SAY SO.

BA BOOM
KISH
BOOM
DING
BOOM

YAP YAP YAP YAP YAP YAP YAP
WHY DO PEOPLE INSIST ON HAVING ANNOYING RINGTONES?
I DON'T KNOW, BUT WHAT CAN YOU DO ABOUT IT?

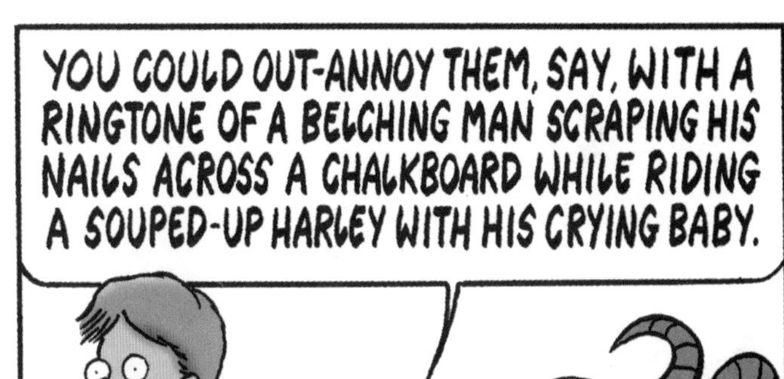
YOU COULD OUT-ANNOY THEM, SAY, WITH A RINGTONE OF A BELCHING MAN SCRAPING HIS NAILS ACROSS A CHALKBOARD WHILE RIDING A SOUPED-UP HARLEY WITH HIS CRYING BABY.

UUUUURRRP
EEEEEEEEEEEEEEEEEEL
VARROOOOM
WAHHHH

PARDON ME. I HAVE A CALL.

WHY DO WE HAVE TO CLEAN OUT OUR STUPID CATCH-ALL DRAWER ANYWAYS?
BECAUSE IT'S BEEN SO LONG WE DON'T EVEN KNOW WHAT'S IN THERE.

WHADDYA MEAN WE DON'T KNOW? EVERYONE'S CATCH-ALL DRAWER HAS ALL THE SAME STUFF...OLD LIGHTER...DEAD BATTERY...STRANGE KEY....

5/21

ADMITTEDLY, THE AMISH MAN WAS A BIT UNUSUAL.

WHO'S YOUR FRIEND, PIG?
JEAN CLAUDE THE HORSE. HE'S A WORLD FAMOUS SCULPTOR AND THAT'S ONE OF HIS MASTERWORKS. BUT BE CAREFUL. IT'S SUPER DELICATE.

LET ME JUST HOLD IT.
PUT IT DOWN! PUT IT DOWN!

BLAM
BLAM
BLAM
THUD
5/22

WELL NOW THAT WAS AN UNFORTUNATE EXPRESSION.

IF YOU COULD EITHER FLY OR BE INVISIBLE, WHICH WOULD YOU PICK?
I'D BE INVISIBLE.

HOW COME?
BECAUSE WHEN I FLY, THEY NEVER GIVE ME ENOUGH PEANUTS.
5/23

NEVER MIND.
AND WHAT'S WITH THE LUGGAGE RESTRICTIONS?

HERE'S YOUR MAIL, PIG. ALL JUNK, I'M AFRAID. CATALOGS, CREDIT CARD OFFERS, COUPONS...
THAT'S OKAY, MAILMAN MIKE... JUST PUT IT ON THE PATH THERE.
5/24

THE PATH? SURE, IF YOU WANT. BUT I DON'T KNOW WHY YOU'D —

FOOOSH

SORRY ABOUT THE SLEEVE.
WANT HIM TO BURN THE STUFF IN YOUR TRUCK, TOO?
UH. NO THANKS.

HEY THERE, PIG... I RUSHED RIGHT OVER WHEN YOU TOLD ME YOU HAD SOME GREAT NEWS.
I DO, BUT IT'S NOT GOOD.
5/25

YOU SAID IT WAS GREAT.
GRATE. I BOUGHT THE WRONG SIZE FOR MY BARBECUE.

EVEN I'M BEGINNING TO HATE YOU.
S. PASTIS

WHAT DO YOU HAVE THERE, RAT?
WEDDING PRESENT. I HAVE TO GO TO ONE OF MY STUPID COUSINS' WEDDINGS.

YOU LEFT THE PRICE TAG ON.
I DID? THEN I PROBABLY DIDN'T NEED TO INCLUDE THAT NOTE.

'HEY, MORONS... I SPENT $125 ON YOUR WEDDING PRESENT.'
5/26

I LIKE MY GENEROSITY TO BE NOTED.

Apologies to the great Jerry Scott and Jim Borgman, who I'm really hoping won't sue me.

MY STUPID KNOW-IT-ALL COUSIN FROM NEW ORLEANS WANTS TO VISIT ME... HE'S THAT GUY WHO EVEN WHEN HE ASKS A QUESTION JUST DOES IT SO HE CAN SHOW YOU WHAT HE KNOWS.

ISN'T HE THAT ONE FROM THE GARDEN DISTRICT WHERE ALL THE WEALTHY TOBACCO, COTTON AND SUGAR MERCHANTS BUILT THEIR HOMES ALONG ST. CHARLES AVENUE IN THE 1840s AND '50s WHEN NEW ORLEANS WAS THE SECOND BIGGEST PORT IN THE UNITED STATES?
5/28

ISN'T SUGAR THE THING I'M ABOUT TO JAM UP YOUR NOSE?
CHECK PLEASE.
YES! YES! THAT IS SUGAR!

HEY, DAD, I KNOW YOU THINK AMPHIBIANS ARE SHIFTY AND UNTRUSTWORTHY, BUT I WANT YOU TO KNOW I'VE BECOME FRIENDS WITH ONE. HE'S FREDDY THE FROG, AND I'D LIKE YOU TO TREAT HIM WITH RESPECT.
BEER

SHAKE
SHAKE
SHAKE
SHAKE
SHAKE
BEER
5/29

Just making sure he no steal silverware.
BEER

So, amphibian... You is start life wid tail, live underwater. Den one day – POOF – you lose tail, live on land... How you essplain?
I DUNNO. I GUESS JUST EVOLUTION. HOW WOULD YOU EXPLAIN IT?

Mebbe you worship Satan?
5/30

OKAY, DAD, TIME TO GO.
Show us you horns, leetle devil frog.

WHAT ARE YOU READING, GOAT?
'OF MICE AND MEN'....IT'S THE STORY OF TWO FRIENDS. ONE IS SHORT AND CRAFTY AND THE OTHER IS AN OVER-SIZED FELLOW WITH MENTAL CHALLENGES.

DO WE GET ROYALTIES FOR THIS?
NO.
I'M FAMOUS! I'M FAMOUS!!
5/31

I GOT A GERMAN SHEPHERD.
HEY, GOOD FOR YOU, PIG. IS HE HOUSE-TRAINED?

ARE YOU HOUSE-TRAINED?
JA.
6/1

THAT WAS PROBABLY INSULTING.

BEHOLD! I, RAT, HAVE INVENTED THE "BOX O' SUPERIOR WISDOM."... REACH IN AND GRAB BRILLIANCE!
Box o' superior wisdom

IT'S BEER.
YES. DRINK EIGHT AND YOU'LL THINK YOU KNOW EVERYTHING.
Box o' superior wisdom
BEER
6/2

THAT IS NOT WISDOM.
Ohhhhhhh? WELL, LISTEN ME TO YOU, WISTER MISE GUY.....
ANOTHER SATISFIED CUSTOMER.

"My husband was supposed to meet me here," she said, "but he's an hour late."

"He's always an hour late. Always. Doesn't call. Nothing. That is, when he even remembers me."

"Of course, if it's his friends, it's different," said Rita Rabbit. "Then he drops everything."

"It's just so frustrating, Elly Elephant. To be married, but so alone. What would you do if you were me?"

Elly Elephant crushed the Marriage Fairy with the sugar dispenser.

HI, JUNIOR. WHAT ARE YOU WATCHING?
FREDDY THE FROG. HE AND HIS FAMILY ARE MOVING IN ACROSS THE STREET.

REALLY?... I DON'T THINK WE'VE HAD AMPHIBIANS ON THE BLOCK BEFORE.
I KNOW, MOM. WHICH IS WHY WE NEED TO DO EVERYTHING WE CAN TO MAKE THEM FEEL AS WELCOME AS POSSIBLE.

BOOOOOOOO.
BEER
BEER
BEER
BEER
6/4

MAKE DAD GO INSIDE.
WHERE YOU TAIL, FORMER FISH??
BEER

LISTEN, DAD, YOU NEED TO ADJUST TO THE FACT THAT WE'RE GONNA HAVE AMPHIBIANS LIKE FREDDY LIVING ACROSS THE STREET.
Okay. Me learn adjust.
THANKS, MR. LARRY.

6/5

PUTTING ON BLINDERS IS NOT ADJUSTING TO FREDDY.
Freddy? Who dis Freddy?
OVER HERE, MR. LARRY.

WHAT DO YOU HAVE THERE, RAT?
A PERSON. I GOT HIM AT THE PERSON STORE.

IS HE HARD TO CARE FOR?
NOT REALLY. YOU JUST GIVE HIM A FLATSCREEN AND ESPN AND HE'LL SIT THERE FOR HOURS.
6/6

WANT TO GIVE HIM A TREAT?
BEER
BEER
BEER

RAT GETS A PERSON PET

FLUSH

IT'S NICE WHEN THEY'RE HOUSE-TRAINED.

I'M TRYING TO FIGURE OUT IF I SHOULD STILL BUY GAS AT THAT PLACE ON MY CORNER.
I THOUGHT THAT WAS A CAR WASH.

IT USED TO BE. NOW IT'S JUST AN EXPENSIVE GAS STATION. I CAN DRIVE TO A CHEAPER ONE FIVE MILES AWAY, BUT THAT MAKES ME USE MORE GAS.
SO IS THE CLOSE GAS STATION CHEAPER?

I THINK IT'S A WASH.
YOU SAID IT WAS A GAS STATION.

CAN WE DISCUSS THIS LATER?
SURE. RIGHT NOW YOU SOUND PRETTY CONFUSED.

HAPPY BIRTHDAY, GOAT! I GOT YOU A GIFT CARD FROM 'STARBUCKS'! DRINK ALL THE MOCHAS YOU WANT.
WELL, GOSH, RAT... THANK YOU!... BUT ALL I WANT?... HOW MUCH MONEY DID YOU PUT ON IT?

NONE. I JUST GOT YOU THE CARD.

YOU'RE A BIT OF AN INGRATE.

HEY THERE, PIG...YOU LOOK HAPPY.
I AM! I JUST MEASURED MYSELF. I'M FIVE FEET, NINE INCHES TALL!

GEE, PIG...THAT SOUNDS A LITTLE HIGH.
WELL, I DID MEASURE MYSELF WITH SHOES.

EVEN WITH SHOES, THAT SOUNDS HIGH.
HERE, MEASURE FOR YOURSELF. I'LL STAND AGAINST THAT FENCE.

6/10

I THINK I SEE THE PROBLEM.
YOU MISJUDGED? IT'S OKAY. WE ALL MAKE MENTAL BOOBOOS.

Hey, son...Where my wife? Me want her sign petition against sheefty amphibian thieves moving eento neighbahood.
SHE'S AT THE HAIRDRESSER, DAD...AND FREDDY'S FAMILY ARE NOT THIEVES... THEY'RE—

AH!
HE STEAL WIFE HAIR!

EXCUSE US, JUNIOR. I'D LIKE TO TALK TO YOUR DAD.
Why you blame me? He one make you look terrible.
6/11

HEY, RAT, I'M HOME!
WHERE YOU BEEN?

GROCERY STORE...DID YOU KNOW THEY HAVE SPRAYERS NOW THAT GO OFF IN THE PRODUCE SECTION?
YEAH. THEY'RE FOR KEEPING THE PRODUCE FROM WILTING.

THAT'S WHAT THEY'RE FOR?
YEAH. WHY?
6/12

NO REASON.

I HEAR YOU'RE UPSET ABOUT YOUR NEW FROG NEIGHBORS.
Yeah. Me hate slimy amphibians almost as much me hate you.

WELL, THE REASON THAT THEY'RE 'SLIMY' IS THAT THEY BREATHE THROUGH THEIR SKIN. IF THEIR SKIN ISN'T MOIST, THEY CAN'T DO THAT.
6/13

WHY ARE YOU BLOW-DRYING FREDDY?
Ohh, juss styling hair.

GOSH, THAT WOMAN SITTING NEXT TO ME SURE IS PRETTY.
WELL, SAY SOMETHING TO HER. NOTHING'S GONNA HAPPEN IF YOU JUST SIT THERE.

EXCUSE ME, BUT DID YOU KNOW THAT THE CHILDREN'S SONG, 'RING AROUND THE ROSIE, A POCKETFUL OF POSIES, ASHES, ASHES, WE ALL FALL DOWN,' IS ACTUALLY A REFERENCE TO THE BLACK DEATH, A PLAGUE THAT KILLED MILLIONS?
6/14

PERHAPS SILENCE IS THE BETTER APPROACH.

DO YOU HAVE ANY ASPIRATIONS IN LIFE?
I AM A REALIST. AND AS A REALIST, I MOCK THE LOFTY ASPIRATIONS OF OTHERS AND MAINTAIN FOR MYSELF BUT ONE SIMPLE GOAL.

WHICH IS WHAT?
TO BE SO GREAT THAT WHEN I DIE, THE WORLD ENDS.
6/15

TRY HUMILITY.
IN THE RACE FOR GREATNESS, HUMILITY IS BUT A BOOBY PRIZE.

WHAT'S THIS COUCH DOING OUT HERE ON THE CURB?
IT'S NEIGHBOR BOB'S. IT'S HOW HE GETS RID OF STUFF HE DOESN'T WANT. A LOT OF PEOPLE DO IT.
Free

IT'S JUST THAT EASY?
YUP.
Free
6/16

SOME THINGS I JUST SHOULDN'T MENTION.
FREE

HEY, RAT, I'D LIKE YOU TO MEET MY FRIEND, HANNAH HIPPO.
HEY.
WELL, HELLO...I'D LOVE TO CHAT MORE, BUT I SIMPLY *MUST* BE LEAVING.
6/17

DIDN'T SHE SAY SHE WAS LEAVING?
OH, THAT'S JUST HANNAH'S WAY. SHE'S THE HIPPO WHO SAYS GOODBYE, BUT NEVER LEAVES.

I HATE THAT...WHEN YOU SAY GOODBYE, GET OUT. DON'T LINGER. LEAVE. YOUR CHAT PRIVILEGES ARE REVOKED.
I HAVE EARS, YOU KNOW...I DON'T NEED TO STAY HERE AND BE INSULTED.
FINE
FINE

DO WE NEED TO RENT A CRANE?
OH. I HEARD THAT. AND I AM SO OUT OF HERE.
MORE COFFEE?
SURE.

YO, DUDE, WHAT ARE YOU DOING HERE?
I TOLD PIG I HAD SOME GREAT NEWS ABOUT A COUSIN OF MINE GETTING MARRIED, AND HE SAID TO COME OVER 'CAUSE HE HAD SOME GREATER NEWS.

YEAH. I GOT A NEW ONE.
6/18

GRATES ON YOU, DOESN'T HE?
GOING HOME NOW.
STAY! SHRED SOME CHEESE!

Whuh you doing, Larry?
Me selling house, Bob. Amphibians ruin neighbahood.
Fore SayLe

But dey juss frogs, Larry. Dere easy way turn dem eento someting else.
Whuh dat?
Fore SayLe
6/19

Kissy, kissy, fairy tale frog.
I'M FEELING VERY UNCOMFORTABLE.

DAD! WHY ARE YOU TRYING TO KISS FREDDY?!
BOB SAY IN FAIRY TALE IT MAKE FROGS BECOME BOOT-IFUL PRINCESS!

THAT'S NOT HOW THE FAIRY TALE GOES, DAD! AND WHY WOULD YOU WANT A BEAUT-IFUL PRINCESS ANYWAYS?... WHAT'S WRONG WITH MOM?

Has you seen new haircut?
6/20

WHAT'S THAT YOU SAY, LARRY?
AHH!
ME LOVE BAD NEW HAIR!
ME LOVE BAD NEW HAIR!

DO YOU THINK IF WE'RE BAD IN LIFE, WE REALLY GO TO A PLACE CALLED 'HELL'? AND IF SO, WHAT'S IT LIKE?

HELL IS A SMALL, WINDOWLESS ROOM FILLED WITH NOTHING BUT THE SOUND OF POLKA MUSIC.

I WILL REPENT RIGHT NOW!
REMEMBER... ONLY SATAN COULD HAVE INVENTED THE ACCORDION.
6/21

Dere is frog. You sure if me kees, he become bootiful princess?
ME SURE. ME SURE. KEES NOW.

SMOOOOOCH
6/22

We got probbum, Bob.
BEHOLD, THOUGHT PRINCE VALIANT, AN UGLY DRAGON TO SLAY.

WHERE'S RAT TODAY?
PRACTICING HIS SKI JUMP POSE. HE'S GONNA USE IT WHENEVER SOMEONE BORES HIM, AS IF TO SAY, 'I'M LEAPING RIGHT OVER YOUR TIRESOME CONVERSATION.'

THAT'S RIDICULOUS. WHY DOES THE GUY HAVE TO BE SUCH A WEIRDO? WHY CAN'T HE JUST BE NORMAL NOW AND THEN?
6/23

THE 'FAMILY CIRCUS' KID?
YEAH. HE JUST RAN OVER FROM THEIR SUNDAY STRIP AND STARTED PUNCHING ME.
ARE OUR PANELS IN THE RIGHT ORDER NOW?
WHO KNOWS? I TRIED TO PUT THEM BACK TOGETHER THE BEST I COULD.
WHY WOULD HE DO THAT?
I DON'T KNOW. HE JUST KEPT SAYING...
WELL, WHERE'S THAT IDIOT NOW?
HE RAN TO ASK HIS MOMMY SOMETHING.
ASK HER WHAT?
"THIS'LL TEACH YOU LITTLE 'PEARLS' PUNKS TO @#☆# WITH THE F.C."
WHAT HAPPENED TO YOU?
JEFFY KEANE BEAT ME UP.
HE SAID THAT?
YEAH. AND THAT WASN'T EVEN THE WORST PART. AFTER THAT, HE RIPPED ALL THE PANELS OF OUR STRIP APART AND THREW 'EM TO THE GROUND.
"Do I need forgiveness for #%&*#%* up a pig?"

I JUST MET THE PRETTIEST GIRL. SHE HAD LONG BROWN HAIR WITH ONE LOCK HANGING DOWN IN FRONT OF HER FOREHEAD.
SOUNDS BEAUTIFUL. I'D LIKE TO MEET HER.

YOU'RE AN EMBARRASSMENT TO THE ART FORM.

HEY THERE, DINKY DUCKLING. HOW COME YOU'RE NOT WITH YOUR MOTHER?
I CAN'T FIND HER. I'M STARTING TO THINK SHE'S ABANDONED ME.

WHY WOULD YOU SAY SUCH A THING?
I FOUND THIS NOTE.

I ABANDONED YOU.

I'D CALL THAT PRETTY VAGUE.
YEAH. SHE JUST THREW IT AT ME AND RAN.

I REALLY DON'T THINK YOUR MOM WOULD ABANDON YOU, DINKY DUCKLING. I'M SURE SHE JUST LOST TRACK OF YOU.

THAT COULD MEAN ANYTHING.

YOU LISTEN TO ME, LARRY...YOU BETTER GET USED TO MY NEW HAIR BECAUSE I LIKE IT.
Yeah, well, Larry NO like. Larry like BEEG hair. Why you cut short?

BECAUSE IT'S IN STYLE...I GOT THE IDEA FROM A VERY CLOSE FRIEND.
Yeah? Well, you tell dat person Larry NO like... Larry tink BAD.
6/28

"He said what??"

LISTEN, DINKY DUCKLING...YOUR MOM HAS NOT ABANDONED YOU...I'M SURE SHE'D BE THRILLED IF YOU FOUND HER.

6/29

WELL, THOSE ARE ODD-LOOKING DUCKS.

HEY, GOAT...WANT TO HELP ME WRITE MY EPITAPH? RAT AND I ARE TRYING TO PLAN AHEAD BY PRE-PURCHASING OUR GRAVESITES AND WRITING OUR OWN EPITAPHS.
WELL, THAT'S GOOD...ONE LESS THING FOR YOUR FAMILY TO WORRY ABOUT.

YEAH, BUT WRITING YOUR OWN EPITAPH IS HARD. SO FAR I'VE TRIED 'LOYAL FRIEND' AND 'GOOD SON,' BUT I DUNNO...I MEAN, HOW DO YOU SUM UP YOUR LIFE IN JUST A FEW WORDS?
6/30

KICKED MAJOR FANNY

Hullooo zeeba neighba... Leesten... You no tink crocs smart, right?
RIGHT.

Yeah, you probably right about— HEAVENS OF BETSY! EES SMARTEST GUY EVER, ALAN EINSTEIN! Me not know you was croc, Alan Einstein!
Why yes me is.

STOP, STOP, STOP... OKAY, FIRST OFF, HIS NAME WAS ALBERT, NOT ALAN. SECOND, DO YOU EVEN KNOW ONE THING ABOUT HIM?

He eenvent blender.
NO. ALBERT EINSTEIN DID NOT INVENT THE BLENDER.

Toaster?
Sticky notes?
HAM??

NO! NO! NO! ALBERT EINSTEIN FORMULATED THE THEORY OF RELATIVITY! $E=MC^2$! AND YOU KNOW WHAT ELSE ABOUT ALBERT EINSTEIN? HE'S DEAD! DEAD! SO WHAT ARE YOU GONNA SAY NOW?!

Ack.
7/1

Great... Now you keel Alan Einstein.
ALBERT
Inventing ham took lot out of me.

HOW COME EVERYONE WHO DOES A 'LISTENER COMMENTARY' ON N.P.R. SOUNDS LIKE A SNOOTY ELITIST THAT NEEDS TO BE PUNCHED IN THE HEAD?
WHAT ARE YOU TALKING ABOUT? THOSE ARE SMART, THOUGHTFUL PEOPLE. IN FACT, I DID ONE OF THOSE ONCE.

CRACK
7/2

I'M GUESSING IT WAS SNOOTY.

HEY, GOAT, WHAT ARE YOU DOING?
JUST DRINKING SOME WINE AND LISTENING TO A PODCAST OF TERRY GROSS' 'FRESH AIR'... IT'S TERRIFIC.

AH, MORE N.P.R.... I'D LIKE TO LISTEN, BUT I'M NOT AS SPECIAL AS YOU.
OH, WILL YOU GET OFF ALL THIS 'ELITIST' CRAP? N.P.R.'S A GREAT STATION THAT COVERS EVERYTHING... EVERYTHING.

MONSTER TRUCK RALLIES?
7/3

OKAY, THERE ARE LIMITS.
HAVE A BEER. WE COMMONERS ENJOY IT.

GOSH, THIS BOOK ON CHARLES DARWIN IS GREAT... IT GETS PAST ALL THE CONTROVERSY SURROUNDING HIS THEORY OF NATURAL SELECTION AND JUST EXPLAINS IT.
WHAT'S NATURAL SELECTION?
7/4

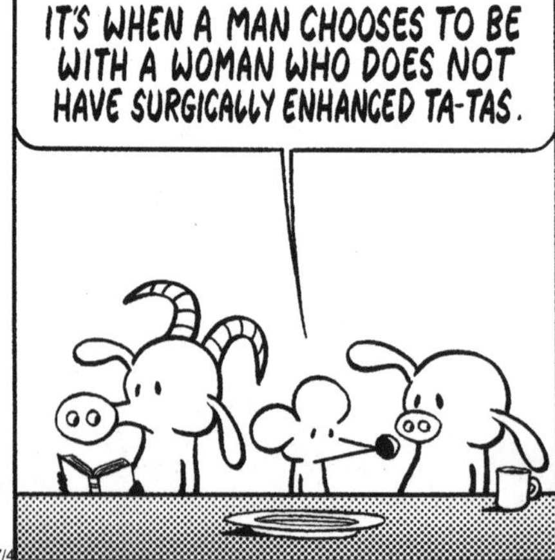
IT'S WHEN A MAN CHOOSES TO BE WITH A WOMAN WHO DOES NOT HAVE SURGICALLY ENHANCED TA-TAS.

NO WONDER IT'S CONTROVERSIAL.
IT'S A VERY TOUGH CHOICE.
STOP!!

WHAT ARE YOU DOING, RAT?
I HAVE MOVED TO AN ISLAND.

WHAT FOR?
TO FOREVER SEPARATE MYSELF FROM THIS WORLD THAT I HATE. SO GOODBYE, GOOD FRIEND, UNTIL WE MEET AGAIN IN A BETTER PLACE.

STUPID TIDE.

EXCUSE ME, EVERYONE...I HAVE AN ANNOUNCEMENT TO MAKE...I JUST GOT BACK FROM THAT NEW CAFE DOWN-TOWN. THEY HAD THREE DIFFERENT SIZES OF COFFEE CUPS. AND THEY HAD LIDS.
SO WHAT, PIG?.. EVERY COFFEE PLACE HAS LIDS.

THE SAME LID FIT ALL THREE CUPS!!

THIS IS WHY WE SHOULD LOCK HIM IN HIS ROOM.
HAS THE NOBEL PRIZE EVER BEEN SUCH A LOCK?!

DO YOU THINK EACH OF US HAS FREE WILL?
NO. ONLY SOME OF US.

WHY DO YOU SAY THAT?
BECAUSE NOT EVERYONE BOUGHT THE DVD.

FREE WILL, NOT 'FREE WILLY.'
OH, GREAT. IS THAT SOME BORING RE-MAKE?

WHAT ARE YOU DOING, GOAT?
I'M PUTTING TOGETHER A BOOK OF FAMOUS WATERWAYS, BUT I'M HAVING TROUBLE GETTING GOOD SHOTS OF THE BERING STRAIT.

NO ONE HAS ANY GOOD PHOTOS?
WELL, THIS ONE PHOTO-COLLECTING GEEK HAS OFFERED TO EMAIL ME SOME, BUT THEY'RE ALL GIFs, AND I LIKE JPGs.
7/8

WHAT ARE THOSE?
THEY'RE JUST DIFFERENT WAYS TO COMPRESS IMAGES ON THE WEB. I LIKE THE COLOR IN JPGs BETTER, SO I WANT TO BE CAREFUL TO NOT USE ANY GIFs.

I GUESS THAT'S WHY YOU HEAR THE WARNING.
WHAT WARNING?

BEWARE OF GEEKS' BERING GIFs.

IT HAD TO BE DONE.
PASTIS
1968 - 2012
Stabbed with his own drawing pen

WHEN ARE YOU GONNA FIND THAT STUPID DUCKLING A HOME?
I'M TRYING MY BEST, BUT WE DON'T KNOW WHERE HIS MOM IS, AND I CAN'T FIND ANYONE ELSE TO TAKE CARE OF HIM.

7/9

I DENY EVERYTHING.

HOW COME AFTER A HOLIDAY WITH MY FAMILY, I ALWAYS FEEL WORSE ABOUT MYSELF?
OH, PIG, I'M SURE THEY DON'T MEAN TO DO THAT... THEY PROBABLY JUST—

BECAUSE LIFE IS LIKE ATTENDING A FOOTBALL GAME. YOUR FRIENDS ARE THE ONES YOU GO TO THE GAME WITH. YOUR FAMILY ARE THE WEIRDOS YOU FIND SITTING AROUND YOU.
7/10

SO THOSE ARE THE FAT PEOPLE THROWING BON BONS AT ME.
PIG, THAT'S NOT—
YEAH. SO BLOW *THIS* IN THEIR FACE.

I'VE CONCLUDED THAT I'M NOT VERY ARROGANT.
HOW'D YOU REACH THAT CONCLUSION?

BY USING MY GINORMOUS BRAIN.
7/11

NEVER MIND.
I'D BE A LOT MORE HUMBLE IF I HAD A REASON TO BE.

ARE YOU A DEMOCRAT OR A REPUBLICAN?
NEITHER. I REALLY PREFER SOME OF THE FRINGE PARTIES. I JUST WISH MORE PEOPLE WANTED TO JOIN ME.

I WOULD LOVE TO COME TO YOUR FRINGE PARTY!!

PLEASE SIT DOWN, PIG.
YOU KNOW, HIS VOTE COUNTS THE SAME AS YOURS.
WILL THERE BE MUSIC AT YOUR FRINGE PARTY?
7/12

ALRIGHT, PRIVATE...IF YOU'RE GONNA BE IN MY ARMY, YOU HAVE TO LOOK THE PART... HALF OF WARFARE IS INTIMIDATION.
OH, I KNOW. SO I WENT OUT AND BOUGHT MYSELF SOMETHING.

PERMISSION TO TOSS HIM IN THE BRIG, SIR?
DENIED.
7/13

HEY, GOAT...I WAS READING YOUR BLOG AT HOME TODAY, BUT I GOT DISTRACTED.
YEAH, THAT CAN HAPPEN WITH EVEN THE MOST COMPELLING WRITING... WHAT DISTRACTED YOU? A PHONE CALL? PERSON AT THE DOOR? TV SHOW?

A BEIGE WALL.

YOU MIGHT WANT TO SPICE UP YOUR BLOG.
7/14

HEY THERE, GOAT... COME WATCH TV WITH US.

NO THANKS. I HAVE A BOOK TO READ.
WHAT BOOK?
7/15

IT'S ON NATURAL SELECTION. IT EXPLAINS HOW A CHANGE THAT BETTER EQUIPS AN ANIMAL TO LIVE GETS PASSED ON TO ITS DESCENDANTS, THEREBY ALTERING THE SPECIES FOREVER.

I'M SORRY... DO YOU UNDERSTAND WHAT THAT MEANS?

THAT MY KIDS WILL HAVE PILLOWS FOR BUTTS.

NO.
AND A REMOTE CONTROL FOR A HAND?
AND CHEESE POOFS FOR FEET?!

Hey, Bob, I know it's your day off, but Jeff needs that report *ASAP*.

The
Opposite
Of
Laugh
Out
Loud

Danny Donkey went to the park.

A woman approached him.
HELP SAVE OUR TRAIN, SIR. IT'S FOR THE CHILDREN.
Dona tions

Danny Donkey looked up and saw a miniature steam train in disrepair.
7/22

"I will save your train," said Danny Donkey. "And give it a new and shiny track."
YAY

So Danny Donkey spent all his money and fixed the train.

And on the day of the re-opening, everyone cheered the shiny new train.
GRand RE-OPENIN
Yay
Yay
D.D.
YAY
YAY

And watched as it departed the new station and rolled down its shiny new track.
Depot
Yay
Yay
Yay
YAY
YAY

Which now led out of the park.
PARK

And straight to the liquor store.
LIQUOR
YAY
OPEN

"'I HAVE BUILT THE WORLD'S MOST CONVENIENT BEER RUN,' SHOUTED DANNY."
THIS IS YOUR COMMEMORATION OF NEIGHBORHOOD IMPROVEMENT DAY?
NO CHILD SHALL EVER BE THIRSTY AGAIN!!

Dear Sirs,
"Prince Valiant" is a registered trademark of King Features Syndicate. Please cease and desist from all future use.

HEY, RAT. WHATCHA GETTING FOR BREAKFAST?
I'M THINKING ABOUT ORDERING A BUNCH OF BACTERIA THAT'S BEEN THROWN INTO MILK AND ALLOWED TO FERMENT.
MENU
MENU

IT'S CALLED YOGURT.
MENU
MENU
YOG
7/26

I LIKE TO BE PRECISE.
MENU
MENU

HEY, GOAT. WHAT DO YOU WANT TO DRINK?
BREAK DOWN SOME GRAIN IN HOT WATER AND LET A BUNCH OF FUNGI EAT IT AND THEN GIVE ME THEIR WASTE PRODUCTS.
MENU
7/27

IT'S CALLED *BEER*, @☆#@ IT!!
MENU

I LIKE TO BE PRECISE.
MENU

DO YOU REALIZE THAT HALF OF THIS COUNTRY PRONOUNCES THE WORD 'AUNT' *ANT*, WHILE THE OTHER HALF PRONOUNCES IT *AWNT*?

CAN'T WE ALL JUST GET ALONG??!
7/28

HE'S VERY SENSITIVE TO DIVISION.
PIG, THEY'RE NOT SHOOTING EACH OTHER.
JOIN MY CANDLELIGHT VIGIL FOR PEACE, WON'T YOU?
LOVE NOT WAR

WHERE ARE YOU, RAT? YOU PROMISED TO HELP PIG AND ME CLEAN OUT MY GARAGE.

I'M LYING ON MY @#@ WITH A BEER ON MY BELLY.
WHY??

NASA.
NASA?

NASA ISSUED A REPORT SAYING THERE ARE CURRENTLY 47,000 ASTEROIDS THAT ARE BIG ENOUGH AND CLOSE ENOUGH TO POSE A THREAT TO EARTH.
SO?!

SO EVERYTHING'S POINTLESS. GOODBYE.
SO YOU'RE GONNA LEAVE THE ENTIRE JOB TO ME AND—

HE'S CLEARLY LOST ALL PERSPECTIVE.

TRADITION IS THE REASON FOR DOING SOMETHING YOU CAN NO LONGER THINK OF A REASON FOR DOING.

HEY, MOM, WHY DID YOU CUT YOUR HAIR?
TO EXPRESS MYSELF BETTER.

WHAT DO YOU MEAN?
WELL, SWEETIE, PRETEND FOR A MOMENT THAT I WANTED TO TELL YOU THE SECRET OF A SUCCESSFUL LIFE, BUT I HAVE MY OLD HAIR.
8/2

OKAY.
OKAY... THE SECRET OF A SUCCESSFUL LIFE IS

SPEECH BALLOON INTERFERENCE.
THE CURSE OF THE BIG-HAIRED WOMAN.

HI, MOM...IT'S ME, PIG...I'M TIRED OF YOU CONTROLLING MY LIFE, SO I'M GONNA GO OUTSIDE AND DECLARE MY INDEPENDENCE FROM YOU IN A VOICE THE WHOLE WORLD CAN HEAR.

SHE SAID TO PUT ON A JACKET.
8/3

HEY, GOAT, WANT TO SEE AN ANIMATED MOVIE WITH ME AND RAT?
I GUESS. BUT WHY'S RAT CARRYING A BOOK OF RUSSIAN PLAYS?
RUSSIAN PLAYS

BECAUSE ALL ANIMATED MOVIES HAVE SICKENINGLY SWEET ENDINGS. AND ALL RUSSIAN PLAYS END WITH SOMEONE SHOOTING THEMSELVES. SO WHEN THE FILM NEARS ITS SACCHARINE END, I JUST STAND AND READ THE LAST PAGE OF THE PLAY ALOUD, THEREBY KEEPING THE WHOLE UNIVERSE IN BALANCE.
RUSSIAN
8/4

OH, THAT MUST BE HEART-WARMING.
IT IS? THEN LISTEN TO THIS... 'AND IVAN SHOT HIMSELF. THE END.'
AWWW... POOR L'IL IVAN.

YOU ENJOYING THE COAST, PIGITA?
NOT REALLY.

I THOUGHT YOU LIKED IT HERE.
I DO. AND I LIKE STARING OUT AT THE BOATS. I THINK IT'S JUST THE SAND IN MY TOES I DON'T LIKE.

OH.
I'M SORRY. I'M JUST NOT A BEACHY KIND OF GIRL.

WOULD YOU RATHER WALK AROUND THE PORT?
OH, I LOVE PORTS.

8/5

SO YOU'RE MORE OF A PORTLY KIND OF GIRL.

MAYBE WE SHOULD AVOID THE COAST ENTIRELY.

I'VE CONCLUDED THAT LIFE IS FUNDAMENTALLY BAD.
WHY DO YOU SAY THAT?

BECAUSE WE HAVE A TYPE OF MUSIC CALLED 'THE BLUES.'
SO?

SO WE HAVE NOTHING CALLED 'THE HAPPIES.'

READING NOW.
WE DON'T EVEN HAVE THE 'JUST GETTING BY'S'!!

HEY, CHECK IT OUT, RAT...WE'RE SCRUNCHING THE STRIP VERTICALLY.
WHAT FOR?

IT CREATES SPACE ABOVE THE STRIP FOR NEWSPAPER READERS TO WRITE NOTES AND STUFF. THAT WAY, MAYBE A HUSBAND AND WIFE COULD COMMUNICATE WITH EACH OTHER IN THE MORNING WITHOUT HAVING TO WASTE EXTRA PAPER.
WHAT DO THEY NEED TO COMMUNICATE ABOUT?

Honey, Don't read this strip. It's not funny.

OH, THAT WORKED OUT WELL.
HEY! I THOUGHT IT WAS CLEVER!

HEY, NEIGHBOR BOB, I HEAR YOU'RE GETTING MARRIED TOMORROW.

YEP. AND TO RELAX, I'M TAKING ALL MY GROOMSMEN TO PLAY SOME GOLF FOR A LITTLE FRIENDLY WAGER. I COULD REALLY USE THE CASH.
THAT'S GREAT! MAY THE BEST MAN WIN!

WHY YOU ROOTING FOR HIM?

WOW. LOOK AT THAT WOMAN'S GREAT JUGS.
PIG, THAT'S RIDICULOUSLY INAPPROPRIATE. GO SAY YOU'RE SORRY.

SORRY.

FOR WHAT?
I DON'T KNOW.
I GIVE UP.

HEY, RAT, IF YOU'RE GONNA COME OVER AND EAT MY CHIPS, PUT THIS BAG CLIP ON THEM WHEN YOU'RE DONE SO THE CHIPS STAY FRESH.
CONSIDER IT DONE.

GREAT. SO YOU'LL DO IT?
NO. I JUST WANT YOU TO CONSIDER IT DONE SO YOU'LL STOP WHINING LIKE AN OVERSENSITIVE NINNY.

GIVE 'EM BACK.
CONSIDER IT DONE.

WHAT DOES IT MEAN WHEN PEOPLE SAY THINGS AREN'T WHAT THEY APPEAR TO BE?
WELL, TAKE THAT GIRL OVER THERE.

WHAT ABOUT HER?
SHE APPEARS TO BE LISTENING TO MUSIC ON HER iPOD. BUT SHE'S NOT. SHE JUST KEEPS THOSE EARBUDS IN HER EARS TO KEEP LOSERS SHE DOESN'T WANT TO TALK TO FROM TALKING TO HER.

OHHH, THAT'S NOT TRUE, IS —
LA LA LA LALALAA LISTENING TO MUSIC...CAN'T HEAR ANYTHING...

HEY, PIG. WHY'D YOU NEED ME TO COME OVER?
I CAN'T SLEEP.

WHY NOT?
RAT SAID THAT IF YOU'RE BAD IN LIFE, YOU'RE FORCED TO LISTEN TO NOTHING BUT POLKA MUSIC WHEN YOU DIE.

8/12

THAT'S NOT TRUE, PIG. HE JUST SAYS STUFF LIKE THAT TO MESS WITH YOU.
YEAH... HOW SILLY.

NOW YOU GET SOME SLEEP AND I'LL SEE YOU TOMORROW.
THANKS, GOAT... YOU CAN TURN OFF THE LIGHTS ON YOUR WAY OUT.

CLICK

PIG?
GOAT? YOU STILL HERE?

POLKA
POLKA
POLKA
MORE POLKA

OUT!
WHAT? I'M JUST SINGING HIM A LULLABY.
AWAY WITH YE, SATAN! AWAY!!

I WAS TRYING TO FIGURE OUT WHAT IT IS THAT BUGS ME SO MUCH ABOUT YOU, AND I THINK I KNOW THE ANSWER.... YOU'RE CONDESCENDING.
THAT'S NOT CORRECT.
8/13

BUT YOU TRIED YOUR BEST.
PAT PAT PAT

PLEASE DON'T TOUCH MY HEAD.
I'M SORRY. IT'S PROBABLY SORE FROM ALL THAT THINKING.

I DON'T GET IT WHEN PEOPLE SAY SOMEONE'S A 'SITTING DUCK.'
A 'SITTING DUCK' IS JUST SOMEONE WHO'S EASY TO ATTACK. WHY IS THAT HARD TO UNDERSTAND?
8/14

IT'S COUNTER TO MY PERSONAL EXPERIENCE.
GO AHEAD. MAKE MY DAY.

WHAT DO YOU THINK HAS CHANGED THE MOST SINCE YOU WERE A KID, STEPH?
PARENTING. WHEN I WAS A KID, MY PARENTS WOULD LET ME GO OFF ALONE FOR HOURS.
8/15

HECK, I EVEN FLEW CROSS COUNTRY ON MY OWN. LOTS OF KIDS DID. AND NOW, PARENTS NEVER LET THEIR KIDS DO STUFF LIKE THAT. AND WHY NOT? I TURNED OUT OKAY.

NEVER CITE YOURSELF AS AN EXAMPLE OF NORMALCY.
MAYBE YOU FELL AND HIT YOUR HEAD A LOT.

WELL, SIR, I'VE FINALLY FIGURED OUT HOW TO USE PRIVATE DINKY IN MY ARMY. HE'LL BE A SURVEILLANCE DRONE HOVERING HIGH OVERHEAD.
DOES HE KNOW HOW TO FLY?

TOSS

SORT OF.

WOULD YOU SAY MY ABILITY TO ANNOY OTHERS IS BEYOND THAT OF ANYONE ELSE?
ABSOLUTELY.

TOLD YOU I HAVE A SUPERPOWER.

I'M LEAVING.
SEE? MY VERY PRESENCE HAS HURLED HIM FROM THE ROOM.
IT *IS* A SUPER-POWER!

HEY, RAT, WANT TO MEET MY FRIEND, GREG?
WHERE IS HE?

AT THE BOTTOM OF THIS HOLE.
WHAT'S HE DOING DOWN THERE?

HE'S AN UNDERGROUND ARTIST.
MORE DIRT ON THE CANVAS.

8/19

WHY IS THAT BRILLIANT?

BECAUSE YOU WALK THROUGH LIFE NOT KNOWING WHO THE IDIOTS ARE! THAT GIVES THEM THE ELEMENT OF SURPRISE! AND THAT'S HOW THEY RUIN YOUR DAY!

PIG, I'VE MADE A CHOICE... ...ABOUT US. I WOULD LIKE TO BE... UH... IN A WORD... WELL... I'LL JUST SAY IT... CELIBATE!
8/20

YAY! YAY!

YOU'RE FINE WITH THAT?
FINE? I LOVE TO CELEBRATE.

LET'S START OVER.
WHY? JOIN IN!
TOOOOOOOT

HEY, GUYS, WHAT ARE YOU DOING?
PLAYING 'TRIVIAL PURSUIT' AGAINST JIMMY THE JELLYFISH.
8/21

WHY ARE YOU PLAYING AGAINST JIMMY?
BECAUSE JELLYFISH HAVE NO BRAIN.

WHAT'S THE CAPITAL OF TEXAS?
BLUE.
AWW, TOO BAD, JIMMY, YOU LOSE AGAIN.

I MISS MY MOTHER.
YOU'LL BE OKAY, PRIVATE. YOU'RE A SURVEILLANCE DRONE NOW.

HOW DOES THAT HELP?
BECAUSE YOU'RE GONNA SHOW EVERYONE WHO EVER REJECTED YOU HOW GREAT YOU'VE BECOME, HOW IMPORTANT, HOW WORLDLY... HOW...
8/22

TOSS

SOMETIMES IT'S EASIER TO JUST DEMONSTRATE.

HEY, RAT, WHAT'S THAT?
MY NEW INVENTION, THE 'TROUBLE BOX.' IF YOU HAVE TROUBLES, YOU PUT 'EM IN HERE AND THEY'RE GONE FOREVER. GO AHEAD, PUT A COUPLE IN THERE.
Trouble Box

I'm dumb and need affection.

Trouble Box

Hee Hee Hee Hee
Trouble Box
8/23

FIRST I LAUGH AT THEM.
Trouble Box

YOU EVER NOTICE HOW WE SEE MUCH OF LIFE THROUGH THE PRISM OF OURSELVES?
HOW SO?
8/24

WHEN PEOPLE AROUND US DO THINGS, WE ASSUME THEIR MOTIVATION FOR DOING SO MUST HAVE SOMETHING TO DO WITH OURSELVES, WHEN IN TRUTH MOST DECISIONS HAVE NOTHING TO DO WITH US.
THAT'S INTERESTING, BUT I NEED TO GET GOING.

WHY? BECAUSE I'M BORING?

BECAUSE I'LL MISS MY DENTIST APPOINTMENT.
CALL ME 'BORING' AGAIN. I DARE YOU.

Hey, zeeba. You like cooking wid gas or charcoal?
WELL, THAT'S THE GREAT DEBATE, ISN'T IT? BUT I SUPPOSE I'D HAVE TO SAY CHARCOAL.

Gud. Geet on grill.
Eet Zeeba
8/25

Guy never cooperate.
Eet Zeeba
CHARCOAL

Dude,
Have Guard Duck
destroy Pakistan.

Rat should get wasted at Disneyland and punch people in the face!!

Do one where a girl takes off her bikini top. Says, "Glad to get that off my chest."

8/26

PLEASE PLEASE PLEASE
do something with Star Wars where everyone blows up.
STAR WARS ROCKS !!!!!!!

My wife Jessica's 39th birthday is on Friday. Have your strip that day say, "Happy B-Day, Jess!"

MORE CROCS!!!

Less crocs.

KILL ALL YOUR CHARACTERS
P.S. Please give me credit if you use this idea.

HEY, STEPH, I HAD AN IDEA FOR A STRIP... DO YOU TAKE SUGGESTIONS?
NO.
SO THIS IS WHERE YOU GET YOUR IDEAS.

HEY, GOAT, I WAS GONNA ASK YOU TO STAY FOR DINNER, BUT THAT HOMEMADE PASTA I GOT FROM PROFESSOR LUNDQUIST WENT STALE.
IS HE THAT PROFESSOR OF LANGUAGE DOWN AT THE COLLEGE?
8/27

YEAH. HE GAVE ME ALL THIS LINGUINE THAT I JUST LET SIT OPEN ON THE SHELF. I FEEL ABSOLUTELY TERRIBLE ABOUT IT.

SO YOU HAVE LINGUIST LUNDQUIST'S LINGUINE LANGUISH ANGUISH?

I HATE THAT GUY.

WHERE'S PIG TODAY?
GETTING READY FOR A DATE WITH A GIRL HE KNEW YEARS AGO. BUT HE'S WORRIED 'CAUSE HE THINKS HE'S TOO FAT NOW.

POOR GUY. WHAT'S HE GONNA DO?
I TOLD HIM IF HE WANTS TO LOOK THINNER, HE SHOULD WEAR SOMETHING WITH VERTICAL STRIPES.
8/28

I FEEL BETTER NOW.

WHAT'S WITH THIS NEW TREND WITH GUYS KEEPING THEIR SUNGLASSES ON THE BACK OF THEIR HEAD?
YEAH. IT'S A LITTLE STRANGE, BUT WHAT ARE YOU GONNA DO ABOUT IT.

YOU LOOK STUPID.
8/29

THERE'S THAT.

HEY, GOAT...I MADE A NEW FRIEND. HE'S A BOUNCER.
A BOUNCER, HUH? MUST BE PRETTY TOUGH.
8/30

BOUNCE
BOUNCE

NOT REALLY.

Hullooo zeeba neighba. Leesten. Crocs start barber shop. Want haircut?
8/31

I DON'T THINK I'D FEEL COMFORTABLE WITH YOUR BARBER.
Whuh wrong wid barber?

Guy juss lack people skills.

HAVE YOU SEEN ALL THOSE ELECTRONIC SIGNS THE CITY PUTS BY THE SIDE OF THE ROAD TELLING YOU THE SPEED YOU'RE DRIVING?
YEAH. THEY'RE TO MAKE YOU SLOW DOWN.

OH.
'OH' WHAT?

I KEEP TRYING TO SET A SPEED RECORD.
9/1

PLEASE STOP TALKING TO ME.
SO THE NUMBERS ARE NOT SENT TO THE 'GUINNESS BOOK OF WORLD RECORDS'?

HEY THERE, PIG. I HEAR YOU GOT A NEW MATTRESS. MIND IF I HAVE A LOOK?

SURE. IT'S ONE OF THOSE MEMORY FOAM ONES.

9/2

OHHH, THESE ARE SUPPOSED TO BE GREAT. DO YOU LIKE IT?

NO. IT'S BAD.
BAD HOW?

AND REMEMBER THE TIME EVERYONE BUT YOU GOT A VALENTINE AND YOU CRIED ALL THE WAY HOME?

BAD MEMORIES.
OH, AND REMEMBER THE TIME YOU SPLIT YOUR PANTS PLAYING TETHERBALL??